Second Edition

Skillful 3

Listening & Speaking Student's Book

Authors: Ellen Kisslinger and Lida Baker
Series Consultant: Dorothy E. Zemach

D0317186

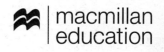

macmillan
education

Grammar	Speaking	Study skills	Unit outcomes
Use past tenses with subordinating conjunctions	Practice expressing interest in ideas you hear Discuss a positive life event that affected your self-identity	Identifying your current skills	Listen for reference to understand main ideas Listen for topic shifts to focus on specific information Plan and present a short description of a positive life event that affected your self-identity
Use *wish* with present or future time	Practice talking about problems and solutions Design and present a new product	Creative problem-solving: difficulties finding a solution?	Practice inferring meaning from context Listen to understand key terms and definitions in context Work in a group to brainstorm, plan, and present a new product designed to solve a problem
Use conjunctions, *may/might/but*, and adverbials to make concessions	Practice responding to an argument Debate the positive and negative effects of technology on academic performance	Organization and memory	Identify claims and supporting evidence to understand arguments in context Listen for repair and elaboration to accurately identify specific information Participate in a group debate on the positive and negative effects of technology on academic performance
Use stance markers	Practice changing the topic and returning to it Debate whether fire does more harm than good	Reviewing notes	Practice distinguishing facts from opinions to help you evaluate arguments Listen for signal words to help you understand the correct sequence of events Participate in a group debate on how fire can be used to benefit or harm us
Use complex passives	Practice voicing and allaying concern Assess and prioritize the risks to public safety in a stadium and suggest solutions	Shortcuts in note-making: using abbreviations	Listen for generalized statements to understand routine and frequency Practice identifying priorities in context Work in a group to assess and prioritize risks in a stadium and present solutions to each issue

	Video	Listening	Vocabulary
6 DISEASE PAGE 98 **Biology** ➤ **Podcast:** Germ myths **Medicine** ➤ **Lecture:** Disease detectives	A buzz in medicine	Listen to categorize information Listen to understand cause-and-effect relationships	Practice and use medical language
7 SURVIVAL PAGE 116 **Sociology** ➤ **Podcast:** Kindness as a survival skill **Architecture** ➤ **Lecture:** Building for the future	Raising awareness	Predict content using prior knowledge Listen for phrases that connect ideas	Practice and use word families
8 LAW PAGE 134 **Crime** ➤ **Podcast:** Cybercrime **Technology** ➤ **Lecture:** Protect yourself online	Crime doesn't pay	Listen to understand supporting evidence: definitions, examples, and explanations Listen to recognize citations	Practice and use legal vocabulary
9 SOUND PAGE 152 **Medical research** ➤ **Podcast:** That's so annoying! **Medical phenomena** ➤ **Radio article:** Was that my phone ringing?	Under the flight path	Listen for organization Listen to interpret the speaker's attitude	Practice and use word + preposition combinations
10 TOMORROW PAGE 170 **Technology** ➤ **Radio discussion:** Drone-free skies **Transportation** ➤ **Lecture:** Hyperloops: the fifth form of transportation	Bat-wing drones	Listen for bias Listen for hyperbole	Practice and use vocabulary for transportation and logistics

Grammar	Speaking	Study skills	Unit outcomes
Use past modals of deduction	Practice asking to clarify or confirm ideas you hear Make deductions about a medical case study and present your findings to the class	Chairing a group	Practice categorizing information to help you understand main ideas Practice identifying cause-and-effect relationships to better understand a text Work in a group to make deductions about how a disease in a medical case study might have been spread and what could have been done to prevent it. Then present your findings to the class
Use present unreal conditionals	Practice contributing additional information to a discussion Discuss the global water challenge and present your ideas to the class	Being effective in group discussion: playing your part	Use prior knowledge to help you predict what you're going to hear Practice identifying main topics and subtopics to better understand text organization Participate in a group discussion about the global water challenge and present ideas about how to save water to the class
Use reporting verbs	Practice disagreeing politely Debate the appropriacy of a punishment in a cybercrime case study	Being a good listener	Practice identifying definitions, examples, and explanations to better understand supporting evidence Listen to identify direct and indirect quotations in context Participate in a group debate about the appropriacy of a punishment in a cybercrime case study
Use cleft sentences	Practice fielding questions during a presentation Design and present a park that allows people to escape noise pollution in the city	Plagiarism	Listen for signal phrases to help you understand text organization Listen for descriptive language to help you identify the speaker's attitude Work in a group to brainstorm, plan, and present a park that allows people to escape noise pollution in the city
Use future perfect progressive	Practice using language for convincing and making persuasive arguments Debate the pros and cons of a future trend towards increased commercial drone use	Planning a persuasive argument	Practice listening for bias to help you better evaluate arguments Listen for hyperbole to help you identify claims not meant to be taken literally Participate in a group debate about the pros and cons of a future trend towards increased commercial drone use

To the student

Academic success requires so much more than memorizing facts. It takes skills. This means that a successful student can both learn and think critically.

Skillful gives you:

- Skills you need to succeed when reading and listening to academic texts
- Skills you need to succeed when writing for and speaking to different audiences
- Skills for critically examining the issues presented by a speaker or a writer
- Study skills for learning and remembering the English language and important information.

To successfully use this book, use these strategies:

Come to class prepared to learn. This means that you should show up well fed, well rested, and prepared with the proper materials. Watch the video online and look at the discussion point before starting each new unit.

Ask questions and interact. Learning a language is not passive. You need to actively participate. Help your classmates, and let them help you. It is easier to learn a language with other people.

Practice! Memorize and use new language. Use the *Skillful* online practice to develop the skills presented in the Student's Book. Revise vocabulary on the review page.

Review your work. Look over the skills, grammar, and vocabulary from previous units. Study a little bit each day, not just before tests.

Be an independent learner, too. Look for opportunities to study and practice English outside of class, such as reading for pleasure and using the Internet in English. Remember that learning skills, like learning a language, takes time and practice. Be patient with yourself, but do not forget to set goals. Check your progress and be proud of your success! I hope you enjoy using *Skillful*!

Dorothy E. Zemach – Series Consultant

Opening page

Each unit starts with two opening pages. These pages get you ready to study the topic of the unit. There is a video to watch and activities to do before you start your class.

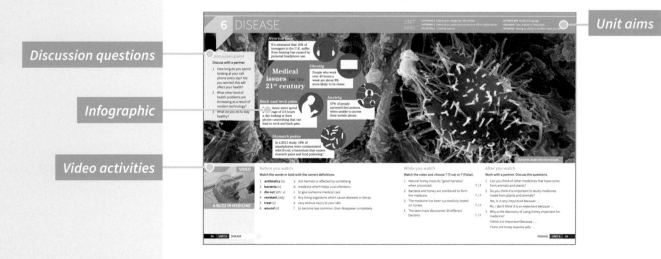

Unit aims

Discussion questions

Infographic

Video activities

Listening lessons

In every unit, there are two listening lessons and they present two different aspects of the unit topic and help you with ideas and language for your speaking task

Vocabulary to prepare you for the listening activities

Develop your listening skills in each part of the listening lesson.

Every listening section helps you use a new listening skill.

Glossaries help you understand higher level words from the listening text.

Speaking lessons

After your listening lessons, there is a page for you to analyze a model answer to a speaking task. This will help you organize your ideas and language and prepare for your final task at the end of the unit.

First, analyze the model answer.

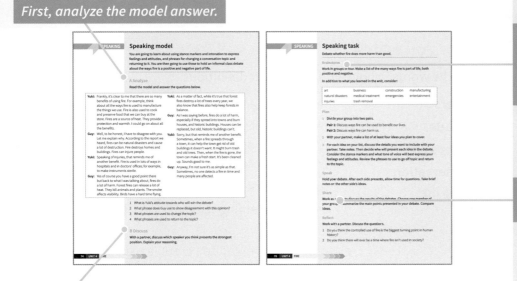

Brainstorm your speaking task and organize your ideas and language from the unit.

Finally, perform your speaking task.

Next, discuss your ideas.

1 IDENTITY

VIDEO

Discussion point

Discuss with a partner.

1 Are you surprised by any of the information in the infographic?

2 What do you think "iris recognition" is and where might it be used?

3 Are you embarrassed by the photo on your ID card or passport?

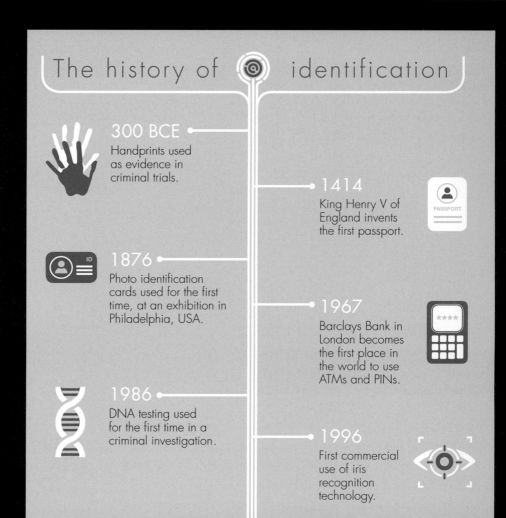

The history of identification

300 BCE
Handprints used as evidence in criminal trials.

1414
King Henry V of England invents the first passport.

1876
Photo identification cards used for the first time, at an exhibition in Philadelphia, USA.

1967
Barclays Bank in London becomes the first place in the world to use ATMs and PINs.

1986
DNA testing used for the first time in a criminal investigation.

1996
First commercial use of iris recognition technology.

VIDEO

KEEPING TRADITIONS ALIVE

Before you watch

Match the words in bold with the correct definitions.

1 **elders** (n)

2 **parade** (v)

3 **percussion** (n)

4 **preservation** (n)

5 **tribe** (n)

a musical instruments, such as drums, that you play by hitting or shaking them

b a group of people who live in the same area and share a common language and customs

c respected older people in a group or society

d keeping something valuable, like a language, culture, or object alive

e to walk as an organized group to celebrate or protest about something

UNIT
AIMS

LISTENING 1 Listening for reference
LISTENING 2 Listening for topic shifts
STUDY SKILL Identifying your current skills

VOCABULARY Suffixes
GRAMMAR Connecting past actions with subordinating conjunctions
SPEAKING Expressing interest in ideas you hear

Researcher working on DNA sequencing.

While you watch

Watch the video. Answer the questions.

1   Where do the people live?

   a   In two tribes, one in Mexico, the other in the United States

   b   In one large tribe in the desert of Mexico

2   What type of people meet to celebrate the customs of the tribe?

   a   Only adults   b   Young and old

3   What do people do in the annual event of celebrations?

   a   Eat and drink   b   Dance and parade through the town

4   What type of things does the local radio station play?

   a   Modern and traditional music, stories, and language lessons

   b   Only traditional music and stories from people of the tribe

After you watch

Work with a partner. Discuss the questions.

1   What annual events, like the one you saw on the video, are celebrated in your town or country?

2   Why is it important for Native American tribes to get together in an annual event?

3   What do you think is the most effective way to keep customs, traditions, and language alive?

Life events

A Vocabulary preview

1 Circle the correct meanings of the words in bold.

1 The college student decided to **major in** computer science.

    a to learn about   b to study as a main subject

2 The class **influenced** the student's decision to major in business.

    a had an effect on   b criticised

3 The student studied hard. This **enabled** him to pass the test.

    a accepted   b made it possible

4 Doing homework with a friend is a way to **combine** socializing and studying.

    a to move toward   b to do two things together

5 Students often say that college helped define their **identity**.

    a who someone is   b a strong human feeling

6 The student wanted to **open up** the discussion to get more ideas.

    a to consider carefully   b to include more people in

7 Working hard can **lead to** success.

    a to decrease   b to make something happen

8 College life **exposed** the student to many new ideas.

    a to show something not   b to give the reason
      previously seen

2 Complete the sentences with words from Exercise 1. Change the form if necessary.

1 It's hard to _____ school and work.

2 Parents shouldn't try to _____ the careers their children decide to have.

3 It's important to protect your _____ online.

4 Not getting enough sleep can _____ poor health.

5 What you _____ doesn't matter. There are lots of jobs.

6 Professors should always _____ discussions to the entire class.

7 College should _____ students to new ideas.

8 The only purpose of college is to _____ students to get a good job.

3 Work with a partner. To what extent do you agree with the sentences in Exercise 2?

B Before you listen

You will hear a seminar in which students discuss events that affected their identity. Check (✓) four events you think students are likely to mention.

- [ ] becoming a student
- [ ] being selected for a sports team
- [ ] taking a very difficult class
- [ ] discovering a personal ability
- [ ] doing well on an entrance test
- [ ] graduating
- [ ] winning an award
- [ ] taking an interesting course

C Global listening

1   🎧 1.1 Listen to *Life events*. Match each student with a defining event and career goal.

Student	Event	Career goal
1 Tom	made the swim team	business
2 Ben	talked to study group	engineering
3 Dan	took some biology classes	journalist
4 Hassan	took a writing seminar	biotech
5 Sonya	the professor was fantastic	sports management

GLOSSARY

biotech (n) the use of bacteria, and plant and animal cells for industrial purposes (e.g. to make drugs and chemicals)

2   Work with a partner. Take turns summarizing what you remember about each of the students.

Tom was … Then he … As a result, he …

Ben planned to … He … After that he …

D Close listening

In lectures and presentations, speakers often use the pronoun *it* to refer back to a noun, phrase, or idea that they introduced earlier:

This <u>article</u> is interesting. You should read **it** for class. (*it* refers to the article.)

<u>The engineering course</u> I took last semester was amazing. **It** changed my life. (*it* refers to the course.)

Speakers also use the following words to refer back: *he / she, him / her, this / that, these / those.*

<u>Dr. Karloff</u> was an excellent lecturer. It was a pleasure to hear **him** speak. (*him* refers to Dr. Karloff.)

<u>Many students said they changed courses after taking a class in another subject.</u> **This** supports my research in the area. (*this* refers to the idea that many students changed course after taking a class.)

The noun, phrase, or idea being referred to may be in the previous sentence, but in a presentation or discussion it might also be several sentences back.

Listening for reference will help you to understand ideas and how they are tied together.

🎧 **1.1** Listen to *Life events* again. Match the word or phrase in bold with the word it refers to.

1 He wanted to be like **them**.

   a students   b father and uncle   c researchers

2 **It's** one from a student named Ben.

   a major   b example   c class

3 **It** was when I made the swim team.

   a example   b defining moment   c major

4 **They** suggested I study business.

   a parents   b professors   c friends

E Critical thinking

Work in a group. Discuss the questions.

1 Which of the life events you heard described do you think had the biggest long-term effect on the person's identity? Explain your reasons.

2 Why are some people more willing to try something new than others?

Study skills — Identifying your current skills

Think about something you do well, a difficulty you overcame, or a personal achievement, no matter how small. It might be success on your exams, skill in a particular sport, learning to drive, or being accepted at college.

Whether your experience is in cooking, riding a bicycle, a sport, or bringing up children, you are likely to have developed a range of strengths that will help you to succeed. The important thing is to recognize which qualities and abilities you already have so that you can draw on them when you need them.

© Stella Cottrell (2013)

1   Complete the table about a personal achievement and what you needed to accomplish it.

Achievement:	
Skills:	
Qualities:	
Attitudes:	

2   Work with a partner. Discuss the questions.

1   Are you surprised to discover how many skills you already have?

2   Can you think of examples of when you underestimated or overestimated your skills?

3   Which qualities and skills do you have that you could adapt to study in higher education?

Beyond the ID card

A Vocabulary preview

1 Match the words in bold with the correct definitions.

1 The man's face was recorded **electronically** and then used to confirm his identity.

2 The student got a passport because his student ID wasn't **sufficient** ID for international travel.

3 The students were offered a **unique** opportunity to visit Italy and were determined to go.

4 The woman's hair and eye color, along with other physical **features** made it easy to identify her.

5 To identify the man, the police used a **combination** of information from a photo and a hair sample.

6 Driver's licenses **vary** from country to country.

7 One way to steal someone's identity is to **pretend** to be that person and apply for a credit card using that person's name.

8 The woman couldn't say with **absolute** certainty that she recognized the man in the photo.

a ___ (n) important parts or aspects of something

b ___ (adv) by means of electronic equipment such as a computer

c ___ (v) to be different in different situations

d ___ (adj) being the only one of a kind, unlike anything else

e ___ (v) to make someone believe that something is true

f ___ (n) two or more different things used together

g ___ (adj) complete or total

h ___ (adj) as much as is needed

2 Complete each sentence with a word in bold from Exercise 1.

1 This is a _____ opportunity we don't want to miss!

2 The photos of the woman _____ from small to large.

3 The images of the men's faces were saved _____.

4 The information you provided was not _____. Please include your address and date of birth.

5 It's against the law to _____ you are someone that you are not.

6 The scientist used a _____ of tests to prove his theory.

7 The man said to the police, "that's the _____ truth."

8 The color of someone's eyes and hair are _____ that can be used to identify the person.

B Before you listen

Work with a partner. Discuss the questions.

1   What types of ID do you regularly use?
2   What kind of information is on your ID card or passport?

C Global listening

1   🔊 1.2 Listen to *Beyond the ID card*. Number the types of identification in the order they are mentioned.

___ DNA testing

___ Photo ID

___ PINs

___ Iris scans

___ Fingerprinting

___ Voice recognition

2   Work with a partner. Discuss the questions.

1   According to the speaker, why do we need more than photo IDs?
2   How does the speaker define biometrics?
3   What is the speaker's opinion about using biometrics as a form of identification?

Listening for topic shifts

D Close listening

Understanding when a speaker moves on to a different topic can help you focus on specific parts of a lecture, presentation, or talk. Listen for these phrases to help you identify when a speaker shifts topic:

Now let's turn our attention to …

Now, let's focus on …

Next, let's consider …

Let's move on to …

1.2 Listen to *Beyond the ID card* again. Circle the correct answer.

1 Which of the following details about photo IDs is NOT mentioned?

  a identification number   c security chip

  b height   d gender

2 According to the speaker, passwords are unreliable because:

  a they can be forgotten.   c they can be changed.

  b they can be too long.   d they can be stolen.

3 According to the speaker, fingerprints are reliable because:

  a they've been used a long time.   c many countries use them.

  b they're easy to do.   d each fingerprint is different.

4 To use voice to identify someone, the person must speak:

  a as loudly as the recording.   c as clearly as the recording.

  b as slowly as the recording.   d the same words as the recording.

5 The disadvantage mentioned of using DNA testing is that:

  a it takes a long time.   c it isn't totally certain.

  b it's expensive to do.   d it must be done in a lab.

6 Why does the speaker mention that "the iris doesn't change over time"?

  a To explain the color.   c To explain why it's flat.

  b To indicate an advantage.   d To show how it's scanned.

E Critical thinking

Work in a group. Discuss the questions.

In addition to crime scenes, what are other places and situations in which the reliability of biometric identification might be useful?

Critical thinking

Recognizing contradiction

Sometimes a speaker presents an argument, a piece of evidence, or an idea that seems to disagree with something else they said. If the ideas presented are so different that they cannot both be true, this is called a **contradiction**.

The development of DNA testing has led to lower crime rates ....

The rise of crime in the area means we need DNA testing more than ever.

(The crime rate cannot be increasing and decreasing at the same time.)

Forty-eight percent of the American public are worried about identity theft ....

Over two thirds of Americans are concerned about having their identity stolen.

(These statistics are different and cannot both be true.)

Recognizing points that contradict each other will help you to evaluate the strength of an argument.

1 Work with a partner. Read the extract from a lecture on iris recognition and answer the questions.

Iris-recognition technology is an incredibly reliable form of identification. In fact, recent studies suggest that it's ten times more accurate than fingerprinting, only producing an incorrect result once every two million tests. It also works with clear contact lenses, glasses, and non-mirrored sunglasses.

However, we should remember that it is still a relatively new technology and many commercial scanners can be tricked by high-quality images of a person's face. For this reason, we cannot rely on iris-recognition software in all situations.

1 What is the contradiction in the extract?

2 Does this strengthen or weaken the speaker's argument? Why?

2 Circle the option that contradicts each sentence.

1 Students waste precious time exploring new ideas.

a Students take required classes their first year.

b Students benefit from taking a variety of classes.

2 Using biometrics is the best way to confirm identity.

a There are limits on the usefulness of biometrics to identify people.

b It's increasingly important to establish people's identity in certain situations.

3 In a group, discuss why it is important to recognize contradiction in society as a whole.

Vocabulary development

Suffixes

A suffix is a group of letters added to the end of a word to change the form or meaning.

Knowing the meaning of common suffixes will help you to develop a rich vocabulary. Some common suffixes and their meanings are:

ADJECTIVAL ENDINGS

SUFFIX	MEANING	EXAMPLES
-ive	having the nature of	creative, expensive
-al	related to	departmental, architectural
-ible / -able	able to be	convertible, washable

NOUN ENDINGS

SUFFIX	MEANING	EXAMPLES
-ation / -tion / -sion	state or result	determination, solution
-ty / -ity / -ility / -ality / -ance	quality of	possibility, accessibility

1   Complete the sentences with the correct suffix.

   1   Police are asking anyone with inform_____ to come forward.

   2   He forgot to write his national_____ on the visa application.

   3   There was a high probab_____ the samples would match.

   4   Voice-recogni_____ software uses the features of a person's voice.

   5   He has consider_____ knowledge about local history.

   6   The situation seemed unmanage_____.

   7   The house has some structur_____ issues.

2   Complete the paragraph with the correct form of each word in the box.

> create   identify   possible   recognize   rely   technology

Confirming someone's [1]_____ can be a particularly difficult thing to do. Although biometric technology has come a long way, there is always the [2]_____ that results will be inaccurate. This is why companies that specialize in biometrics work hard to develop [3]_____ approaches that work every time. For example, one way to identify a person is to analyze their way of walking, or "gait." Recent [4]_____ advancements mean that gait-[5]_____ software is now a fairly [6]_____ way to identify someone.

Academic words

1   Match the words in bold with the correct definitions.

   1   The man relied on his strong family **structure** to provide him with support.
   2   Attending an elite university improved his **status** in the community.
   3   Six students **attained** full marks on the exam.
   4   The lab **established** the identity of the victim using DNA testing.
   5   His **diverse** interests made it difficult to decide on a career.
   6   Applicants must **submit** proposals by Tuesday afternoon.
   7   The lab had to **extract** DNA from several samples for comparison.

   a   (n) the social position of someone in relation to others
   b   (v) to succeed in getting something you want
   c   (v) to give someone a document, proposal, etc. for consideration
   d   (v) to discover, prove, or decide something is true
   e   (n) the ways parts of something connect to form a whole
   f   (v) to remove something from a particular place
   g   (adj) very different from each other

2   Complete the sentences with a word in bold from Exercise 1.

   1   Students must _____ an application for campus housing.
   2   To genetically modify food, scientists _____ DNA from the cell of one plant and transfer it to another.
   3   The _____ of universities varies from country to country.
   4   The company has a _____ workforce.
   5   Some careers lead to a higher_____ in society than others.
   6   After years of hard work, Mishal _____ a medical degree.
   7   The bank _____ his identity using voice-recognition software.

3   Work with a partner. Discuss the questions.

   1   What careers in your country have high status?
   2   What is your family structure like?
   3   What type of personality is needed to attain goals?
   4   What are the advantages of studying in a group of students with diverse backgrounds?

Speaking model

You are going to learn about using past tenses with subordinating conjunctions, expressing interest in ideas you hear, and using intonation to express interest. You are then going to use these to discuss life events that have affected your self-identity.

A Analyze

Alex: So, there are of lots of events that have affected my self-identity, but I want to tell you about a trip that had a positive influence on me when I was younger.

Miki: Oh, right. So, where did you go?

Alex: To the Azores, a group of islands off the coast of Portugal. Before we went there I'd never even heard of them. I really didn't want to go, but the more I read of my parents' travel guide, the more excited I was to go. I realized it was a unique opportunity to learn about another culture.

Miki: So, what happened when you got there?

Alex: As soon as I got there, I realized how different it was from back home. It was so diverse. There were volcanoes, mountains, beautiful beaches …. I just wanted to see and do everything.

Miki: Wow! That sounds amazing.

Alex: Yes, it was. On the first day we were there, we went on a boat tour and saw whales, dolphins, sea turtles …. The day after that we hiked to a volcano called Caldeira. Once we got to the lookout, we had an amazing view of the island. Oh, yeah, and then the following day, we climbed Pico Mountain.

Miki: It sounds like you and your family like to be active! Didn't you ever get tired?

Alex: Definitely, but it was a lot of fun. Before we came home, I went horseback riding too.

Miki: Nice. So, how do you think this trip affected your self-identity?

Alex: Umm … really it just opened up a new world to me. I'd never been exposed to other cultures, and that trip gave me my first taste of the world outside my country. Also, it was on that trip I realized how much I love physical activity. I'd wasted so much time indoors playing video games or watching TV, but after that I started to spend more and more of my time hiking, diving, or rock-climbing.

Miki: Sounds like it was a really positive experience; thanks for telling me about it.

Read the model and answer the questions with a partner.

1 Where did Alex go?
2 Before the trip, how did he feel and why did he change his mind?
3 How did he feel about the trip afterwards?
4 How did the trip affect the student's self-identity?

B Discuss

Work with a partner. Discuss the questions.

1 Does this sound like the kind of trip you that you'd usually go on? Why? / Why not?
2 Have you ever had a cultural experience that changed your world view?

Grammar

Connecting past actions with subordinating conjunctions

When we talk about the past, we can use subordinating conjunctions to show different relationships between events. Common uses are:

To show that one action happened *earlier* than another:
Before I went to college, I'd never left my home town.

To show that one action happened *later* than another:
After I left school, I decided I wanted to go traveling.

To show that one action happened immediately *after* another:
As soon as the class began, I realized I'd chosen the wrong course.

To define a period from a specific time in the past to now:
Since I started college, I have learned many new ideas.

To show that one action happened up to a specific time, then finished:
I waited with her until the bus arrived.

To show that two actions happened at the same time:
While I was studying, my roommate took a nap.

1 Choose the correct conjunction to complete each sentence.

   1 **Until / As soon as** I got to college, I realized I didn't want to study finance.
   2 **Before / When** going to college, I'd never actually left my home state.
   3 My grades began to improve **while / once** I'd moved to a different dorm.
   4 **While / Since** studying at Pennbrook State, I met my future business partner.
   5 **After / Until** speaking to my tutor, I decided to change my major.
   6 I've met such a diverse group of people **while / since** I started college.

2 Complete the second sentence so it has a similar meaning to the first, using the conjunction in bold, and no more than four additional words.

   1 It was almost dark when I left the university. **UNTIL**
   I didn't ___leave university until___ it was almost dark.
   2 My brother became an engineer when he finished college. **SINCE**
   My brother has _____ he finished college.
   3 I went traveling immediately after I had finished my exams. **SOON**
   I went _____ I had finished my exams.
   4 The student didn't eat dinner until he got home. **AFTER**
   The student _____ he got home.

Speaking skill

During a conversation or informal discussion, you can show interest in what other people are saying by:

Making comments

Wow! / Really? / You're kidding! / That sounds interesting.

Repeating part of what you heard

Sorry, you left college after only ten weeks?

Asking follow-up questions

So how did you decide which course to apply for?

Why did you change your major to engineering?

1 Read the conversations and cross out the response that would <u>not</u> be appropriate.

1 A: When I was about 12, I decided I wanted to be a professional photographer. I started taking pictures everywhere I went. I kept that up for about five years, and then I stopped.

B: Why did you stop? / That's a shame. / You're kidding!

2 A: I went to an amazing exhibit at the National History Museum when I was younger. It's really what inspired me to study biology.

B: What was it about? / Really? / I can't believe it.

3 A: So, yesterday I was walking down the street and I saw this guy who looked very familiar, but I wasn't sure who it was. As he got closer, I realized it was my favorite teacher from high school.

B: What a coincidence! / It was a guy you didn't recognize? / How did you know who it was?

4 A: In my first year at college, I was supposed to go on a research trip to Brazil. It would have been amazing, but the night before I was due to leave, I realized I'd lost my passport.

B: So, what did you do? / Oh no! / That sounds interesting.

2 Work with a partner. Student A: Answer the questions below. Student B: Show interest in your partner's answers using techniques from the skills box.

1 What's the most challenging course you've ever studied?

2 Have you ever thought that you might be studying the wrong subject?

3 What are your future career goals?

4 Is there anything else you'd like to study in the future?

5 What was your least favorite subject at school?

Pronunciation for speaking

> ## Using intonation to express interest
>
> Statements in English naturally have *falling intonation*. The speaker's voice goes up on the last stressed syllable of a sentence, then falls:
>
> *When I was 21, I decided to leave college to start my own **bus**iness.*
>
> When speakers want to express interest, they emphasize this fall by using a higher pitch for key words and phrases. This is called a **high fall tone**:
>
> *A: I took a year off college to travel around Japan.* **B:** *That sounds a**maz**ing!*

1   🎧 **1.3** Listen to the pairs of responses. Choose the response that is said with enthusiastic intonation.

   1   a   That sounds amazing.   b   That sounds amazing.

   2   a   Oh, really?   b   Oh, really?

   3   a   That's great.   b   That's great.

   4   a   Me too.   b   Me too.

   5   a   Yes, I have.   b   Yes, I have.

2   🎧 **1.4** Read the conversations. Draw arrows (⌃⌄) to predict where a high fall tone will be used in the responses. Then listen and check.

   1

   A: When I was 17, I became the youngest person ever to study at NSY.

   B: Oh, really? That's amazing.

   2

   A: I taught English in Japan for a year in my twenties.

   B: Me too! Where did you work?

   3

   A: Last summer, a friend and I climbed Mount Everest.

   B: Wow! That sounds incredible. How long did it take?

   4

   A: I traveled around Iceland for a few months after I graduated from college.

   B: It's a beautiful country, isn't it?

3   Practice the conversations in Exercise 2.

Speaking task

Discuss a positive life event that affected your self-identity.

Brainstorm

Work alone. Make a list of positive events in your life that have affected your self-identity.

EVENT	AGE	HOW IT HAS AFFECTED YOU

Plan

Choose one event to talk about. Plan what you are going to say using the speaking model on page 20.

Speak

Practice your answer. Remember to use subordinating conjunctions to connect your ideas.

Share

Work with a partner.

Student A: Tell your partner about the positive event that affected your self-identity.

Student B: Listen and show interest using words and phrases from page 22 and a high fall tone where appropriate.

Swap roles when you've finished.

Reflect

Work in a group. Discuss the questions.

1 How important is it to protect your identity in this digital age?
2 What factors do you think might influence your self-identity in the future?

Review

Wordlist

MACMILLAN
DICTIONARY

Vocabulary preview

absolute (adj) **	enable (v) ***	influence (v) ***	pretend (v) **
combination (n) ***	expose (v) **	lead to (phr v)	sufficient (adj) ***
combine (v) ***	feature (n) ***	major in (phr v)	unique (adj) ***
electronically (adv)	identity (n) ***	open up (phr v)	vary (v) ***

Vocabulary development

accessible (adj)	knowledgeable (adj)	nationality (n) *	recognition (n) ***
information (n) ***	manageable (adj) *	probability (n) **	structural (adj) **

Academic words

attain (v) *	establish (v) ***	status (n) ***	submit (v) ***
diverse (adj) **	extract (v) **	structure (n) ***	

Academic words review

Complete the sentences using words from the box.

attain	diverse	established	status	submitted

1   Essays must be _____ to your tutors by Thursday July 27th.
2   In most countries, being a lawyer is a very high-_____ profession.
3   The forensic team _____ the identity of the body using dental records.
4   Students are expected to _____ high levels of academic achievement.
5   New York is home to people from a _____ range of cultures.

Unit review

Listening 1		I can listen for reference.
Listening 2		I can listen for topic shifts.
Study skill		I can identify my current skills.
Vocabulary		I can use common suffixes.
Grammar		I can connect past actions using subordinating conjunctions.
Speaking		I can express interest in the ideas I hear.

Discussion point

Discuss with a partner.

1 Which of the 10 principles are the most, and least, important?

2 Think of a product you use every day. Does it follow the principles of Dieter Rams?

3 Do you think about design or price when you shop for a new product?

aesthetic (adj) attractive or beautiful to look at

innovative (adj) new and original

principle (n) a basic belief or idea that affects how something is done

thorough (adj) complete; not missing any necessary parts or details

unobtrusive (adj) not attracting too much attention

Dieter Rams'
10 *principles of good design*

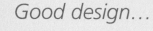

Good design…

1 is innovative

2 makes a product useful

3 is aesthetic

4 makes a product understandable

5 is unobtrusive

6 is honest

7 is long-lasting

8 is thorough down to the last detail

9 is environmentally friendly

10 is as little design as possible

VIDEO

A VIRTUAL FUTURE?

Before you watch

1 Complete the sentences with the words in the box.

gadget	gimmicky	headsets	kit

1 All VR _____ are heavy and uncomfortable.

2 VR is the must-have _____ of this generation.

3 VR is _____ and expensive.

4 VR requires far too much _____.

2 Work with a partner. Do you agree with the sentences in Exercise 1? Why? / Why not?

UNIT
AIMS

LISTENING 1 Inferring from context
LISTENING 2 Listening for key terms and definitions
STUDY SKILL Creative problem solving: difficulties finding a solution?

VOCABULARY Design vocabulary
GRAMMAR *Wish* when referring to present or future time
SPEAKING Talking about problems and solutions

Dieter Rams' portable radio.

While you watch

Watch the video and choose *T* (True) or *F* (False).

1 The Mobile World Congress is held twice a year.   T / F

2 Antonio Muñoz is at the MWC to present a new VR headset.   T / F

3 The default sales kit comes with one base station.   T / F

4 Antonio Muñoz believes his VR headset is worth the money.   T / F

5 It's predicted that 97 billion headsets will have been sold by 2020.   T / F

After you watch

Work with a partner. Discuss the questions.

1 Would you pay nearly 800 US dollars for a VR kit? Why? / Why not?

  Yes, I would because …

  No, not particularly because I think …

2 What kind of games would you like to try or worlds would you like to visit?

  I'd like to try out …

3 What other uses, apart from games, could VR equipment have?

Principles of good design

A Vocabulary preview

1 Match the words in bold with the correct definitions.

1	**come up with** (phr v)	a	to find the size, weight, or amount of something
2	**complex** (adj)	b	to be able to understand something or solve a problem
3	**device** (n)		
4	**features** (n)	c	to use or control a piece of equipment
5	**figure out** (phr v)	d	a machine or piece of equipment used for a specific purpose
6	**functional** (adj)	e	designed to be good at a doing a particular job
7	**measure** (v)	f	involving lots of details or small parts that make it difficult to understand
8	**operate** (v)	g	to think of an idea, plan, or solution
		h	important parts or pieces of something

2 Complete the sentences with the words in bold from Exercise 1.

1 Good design should be simple, never too _____.

2 It's important for any mobile _____ to be attractive, and easy to use.

3 If you can't _____ how something works, it's badly designed.

4 Today's cell phones have too many hidden _____.

5 Working in a group is the best way to invent products, and _____ new ideas.

6 There is no easy way to _____ the success of a product's design.

7 You shouldn't need instructions to _____ new technology.

8 Buy products because they're _____, not because they look good.

3 Work with a partner. Which sentences in Exercise 2 do you agree with, and why?

B Before you listen

Activating prior knowledge

Look at the pictures of everyday objects. Do you think they are well-designed? Why? / Why not?

Norman door

measuring jug

Braun calculator

coffee machine

C Global listening

1 🎧 **2.1** Listen to *Principles of good design,* and number the products in the order they are mentioned.

___ measuring jugs ___ coffee machines

___ the Braun calculator ___ microwaves

___ TV remotes ___ Norman doors

2 🎧 **2.1** Listen to *Principles of good design* again, and choose the correct option to complete the sentences.

1 Dieter Rams was a German …

   a engineer.

   b scientist.

   c designer.

2 The Braun calculator is given as an example of …

   a a poorly designed product.

   b a product designed by Rams.

   c a product that was designed in the 1970s.

3 Don Norman believes doors …

   a shouldn't need written instructions.

   b should always have "push" and "pull" written on them.

   c should all have vertical handles.

4 Marta thinks her coffee machine …

   a is simple, and easy to use.

   b is difficult to operate.

   c doesn't need such a complicated instruction manual.

5 Marta chooses to evaluate … for her assignment.

   a a TV remote

   b a coffee machine

   c a measuring jug

D Close listening

> **Inferring** is the process of drawing conclusions based on information that is implied, but not said directly. By listening for **clues**—the speaker's or speakers' words and tone of voice, as well as your knowledge of the world—you can make inferences about the conversation.
>
> The following are common types of inference questions in exams:
>
> *Who are the speakers? / What are they talking about? / How does the speaker probably feel about …? / What did the speaker mean by …? / Why did the speaker say…? / What can you conclude about…? / It can be inferred that …*

🎧 **2.1** Listen to *Principles of good design* again. Answer the questions.

1   We can infer that the Braun calculator …

    a   is complicated.   c   has a simple design.

    b   has unnecessary features.   d   is no longer in production.

2   We can infer that Don Norman …

    a   thinks designers can ignore the user of their products.

    b   thinks doors are usually badly designed.

    c   is interested in everyday items being simple to use.

    d   thinks products should clearly state how they should be used.

3   Marta's kitchen jug was designed to be most useful for …

    a   holding dry food.   c   measuring hot liquids.

    b   mixing powders.   d   displaying in the kitchen.

4   What can we infer about Marta?

    a   She is a fast learner.   c   She is lazy.

    b   She admires her father's understanding of technology.   d   She lives in university accommodation.

E Critical thinking

Work in a group. Discuss the questions.

1   Have you experienced the problem with doors that Norman describes?

2   How would you design a door that does not require written instructions?

3   How do products in your classroom signal to the user how they should be held, pressed, turned, or moved?

Study skills | Creative problem-solving: difficulties finding a solution?

If the solution to a problem isn't immediately apparent, work creatively to find a different approach.

Simplify

- Remove unnecessary detail.
- Generalize: find points in common with other material or theories you have covered.
- Make broad assumptions that help you generalize the problem.

Consider alternative ways of looking at it

- Take a different angle: rephrase the problem, or look up similar examples.
- Make it real: relate problems to parallel, concrete problems from real life.
- Combine the possibilities: does the problem have several parts to it that each need to call upon a different aspect of previous coursework?

© Stella Cottrell (2013)

Work with a partner. First, practice simplifying the problem, then consider alternative ways of looking at it. Come up with a better solution for each problem.

1 Your school's new library building is very poorly designed, and all the subjects are in different areas. The new library staff members are unsure where to find anything. Many students are wasting a lot of time trying to find books they need, and often leave empty-handed in frustration.

   The school's solution is for new students to be given a tour of the library in their first week on campus.

2 You are taking an exam next week, and you and your classmates are worried you might fail because you are not sure what will be in the exam. Your teacher is away on leave, and hasn't left any revision notes or instructions.

   The school's solution is to remind you to revise carefully using your reading list.

3 The process for handing in assignments at your college is inefficient. Students have to queue at the Dean's office to have the assignment stamped, and then there are so many papers that they often get lost, or grading is delayed. Assignments are often late because queuing takes so long. Students are penalized for late submission.

   The school's solution is to suggest students get up early to be first in the queue.

VR and AR

A Vocabulary preview

Complete the sentences with the words in the box.

artificial	computer-generated	feedback	layer
similarity	simulation	three-dimensional	train

1 This is just one _____ between the two programs.
2 _____ imagery (CGI) is a common feature of modern movies.
3 It's not real though. Players explore an _____ universe.
4 _____ on the game has been generally positive.
5 We used a computer _____ to test our design.
6 The program allows designers to _____ text over the image.
7 Students build real _____ models to explain their design.
8 Laurence has agreed to _____ the new web designer.

B Before you listen

Activating prior knowledge

Work with a partner. Discuss the questions.

1 What are the people doing in the pictures?
2 What do you know about *augmented reality* (AR) and *virtual reality* (VR)?

C Global listening

🎧 **2.2** Listen to *VR and AR*. Complete the outline with the topics in the box in the order that the speaker discusses them.

> aviation   blended AR/VR experience   definition: augmented reality
> definition: virtual reality   fashion   haptic feedback   medicine
> similarity between AR/VR

1   Introduction of speaker, and topic

   1 _____: alter our perception of the world.

   2 _____

   Ex.: Pokémon Go

   3 _____

2   Uses of VR / AR today

   Entertainment

   4 _____

   5 _____

3   AR / VR in the future

   6 _____

   7 _____

   8 _____

Listening for key terms and definitions

D Close listening

Good speakers often provide definitions of key terms in order to help listeners follow the content of their presentation. English has many ways of signaling a definition. For example:

(Note: X = the term being defined)

X means / is …   *X can be defined as …*

X, meaning / which means / which is …   *X, or …*

An X is a [type, or class] that …   *The definition / meaning of X is …*

This term means …

1 🎧 2.3 Listen to part of *VR and AR* again. Complete the definitions with words from the box.

> arachnophobia   augmented reality
> haptic   to augment   virtual reality

1 _____ something means to add to or increase it.

2 _____ is a technology that layers or puts computer-generated content on top of the existing environment.

3 _____, is an artificial, computer-generated simulation—that means a copy—of a real-world environment.

4 Let's say you have a person with _____, which is a fear of spiders.

5 The term "_____" is defined as "relating to the sense of touch."

2 🎧 2.2 Listen to the whole talk again. Write *AR*, *VR*, or *Both* next to each item.

1 _____ alters our perception of reality

2 _____ combines the real environment with artificial images

3 _____ requires a special headset

4 _____ used for entertainment and play

5 _____ used for training pilots

6 _____ used to train surgeons

7 _____ will soon include haptic feedback

E Critical thinking

Work with a partner. Discuss how you think VR and AR technology could be used to improve education.

Critical thinking

Developing and applying evaluation standards

Creating and applying a clear set of standards can help you logically evaluate anything from products to arguments.

For example, think about when you were choosing your current phone. You probably asked yourself questions like – Is it good value for money? Does it have all of the features I want?

This approach could equally be applied to an argument – Does the speaker provide sufficient evidence? Are the sources reliable? Is their conclusion logical?

Taking this methodical approach to evaluation is a simple way to think critically about ideas you're presented with.

1 Look back at *Dieter Rams' 10 principles of good design* on page 26. Discuss the questions with a partner.

   1 What do each of the principles mean?

   2 What do you think Rams used the principles for?

2 Work with a partner. Discuss which of Rams' principles are most / least important for the following products:

   phone   lightbulb   car   computer   shoes

3 Work in a group. Make a list of five principles you could use to evaluate a house or apartment. Then use these principles to evaluate where you live. According to your standards, who has the best house or apartment?

An interior view of an apartment in the Corbusier House in Berlin, Germany.

Vocabulary development

Words to talk about design

1 Match the words in bold with the correct definitions.

1 **classic** (adj)
2 **element** (n)
3 **environmentally friendly** (adj)
4 **flexible** (adj)
5 **image** (n)
6 **industrial** (adj)
7 **measurement** (n)
8 **process** (n)

a able to change, bend, or move easily; or be used for different purposes

b connected with the production of goods in factories, especially using machines

c popular for a very long time because it is very good

d a picture in a magazine, on a computer, etc.

e the size, or amount of something, expressed in numbers, or standard units such as millimeters, or ounces

f a basic part of something

g not harmful to the air, water, earth, etc.

h a set of actions done in a particular order for the purpose of making, or doing something

2 Complete the sentences with words from Exercise 1. Change the form if necessary.

1 Most countries use metric _____, that is centimeters, liters, etc., but the United States uses "imperial" units like inches, and pounds.

2 The _____ Revolution in the 18th and 19th centuries was the time when machines were first used to make products in large quantities.

3 Plastic is a very _____ material. It can be used to make thousands of different things.

4 April 22 is Earth Day, when people celebrate our planet, and honor _____ companies that produce goods without causing pollution.

5 The Chanel Suit is a _____ design that will never go out of fashion.

6 Let me talk you through the key _____ of our design.

7 The camera on the latest smartphone produces incredibly clear and bright _____.

8 The first step in the design _____ is defining a need; that is, thinking of a product or service that should, but does not yet exist.

Academic words

1 Match the words in bold with the correct definitions.

1 **alter** (v)   a to talk, or do things with other people

2 **contrast** (n)   b a large difference

3 **eventually** (adv) c a thing that replaces another, similar thing

4 **income** (n)   d money that someone earns

5 **interact** (v)   e to change

6 **substitute** (n)   f after a long period of time

2 Complete the sentences with the words in bold from Exercise 1.

1 Once I form an opinion, or belief, it is very hard for me to _____ my thinking.

2 I love shoes with colors that have a lot of _____, such as black and white, or red and yellow.

3 _____, after I finish my education, I would like to have a large family.

4 In my chosen profession, most people can expect to make a good _____ after they finish their education.

5 When I travel, I make a great effort to _____ with local people, eat their food, and speak their language.

6 I usually don't use real sugar in my coffee. I prefer to use a _____ like sucralose, or aspartame.

3 Work with a partner. Which of the sentences in Exercise 2 are true for you?

Speaking model

You are going to learn about *wish* when it is used to talk about present time, talking about problems and solutions, and using intonation to make declarative statements. You are then going to use these to design a new product in a group.

A Analyze

Alex: Let's start by identifying a problem that needs to be solved. And then we'll try to come up with a product, or process for solving it. Does anyone have an idea?

Lizzie: I do. Where I live, it rains all the time, and I always get soaking wet.

Alex: That problem has been solved. Get an umbrella.

Lizzie: But umbrellas are terribly designed. They're constantly breaking, and they're dangerous. I wish someone would invent an umbrella that doesn't break, turn inside out in a strong wind, or poke people in the eye.

Sevban: Oh, I agree! I get hit by umbrellas all the time; it's really annoying.

Lizzie: And another problem is that it's a real pain to close most umbrellas. You have to use both hands, and it's hard to fold them up properly.

Alex: You're right. So, we need to design an umbrella that is safe, doesn't break, and that's easy to close up. Any ideas?

Lizzie: I think we could solve the first problem if the umbrella frame were made of plastic instead of aluminum. Plastic is flexible, so the umbrella would bend instead of breaking in the wind. A product like that would be longer-lasting, and much more environmentally friendly.

Alex: What about making it easier to close?

Sevban: I have an idea. You know how a lot of umbrellas have a button you can push so it opens instantly? What if our umbrella had a button you could press to close it instantly? All we'd need is a simple mechanism …

Alex: You could do it with one hand.

Lizzie: That would be really useful.

Work with a partner. Read the model, and answer the questions.

1 What problem is the group trying to solve?
2 What three issues do the students have with umbrellas?
3 What solutions do they come up with?
4 How do the speakers invite each other to share ideas?
5 What phrases do the speakers use to show their frustration with umbrellas?

B Discuss

Work with a partner. Discuss the questions.

1 What other solutions can you think of to solve the problems the students mention?
2 Are there any other ways to solve the problem without having an umbrella?

Grammar

Wish when referring to present or future time

We use *wish* + past simple to talk about things we want to change in the present:

I wish this coat had pockets.

Stella wishes she were a designer.

We use *wish* + *would / could* + base form to talk about things we want to change in the near future:

I wish someone would invent a better umbrella.

I wish we could find a more environmentally friendly solution.

1 Complete the sentences with the correct form of the verb or modal + verb in parentheses.

   1 Today is Tuesday. I wish it _____ (be) Saturday so that I could stay home.

   2 I don't have my classmate's number. I wish I _____ (have) it so I could invite her to a party.

   3 Rada wishes she _____ (can fly) home for the winter break, but she can't afford to buy a ticket.

   4 These shoes hurt my feet. I wish they _____ (be) half a size larger.

   5 My neighbors are too noisy. I wish they _____ (move).

   6 I'm going to be late to work. I wish the bus _____ (come).

2 Work with a partner. Answer the questions. Use *wish* in your responses.

   1 Think of an object you use every day. Do you wish you could change, or improve it? How?

   2 What career will you have in the future? What career do you wish you could have, or be?

   3 Think about the design of your classroom, or school building. What do you wish were different? What do you wish the room or building had?

   4 What skill do you wish you had, or what do you wish you knew how to do?

   5 Imagine that you had your choice of a personal trainer, a personal chef, or a personal driver. Which one do you wish you had?

   6 Do you like the place where you live? Do you wish you lived somewhere else? Explain.

Speaking skill

We use the following phrases to talk about problems and solutions:

Talking about problems	Talking about solutions
One problem is … The second is …	*Why don't we / you …?*
The biggest issue is that…	*How about* verb+*ing?*
The (main / obvious) problem / challenge / difficulty / issue is …	*The (best) solution is …*
	What if we / you …
I have (several / a lot of) problems with …	*I suggest we / you …*
It's a (big / serious) problem.	*What if we / you …*

1   Work with a partner. Take turns describing the problems below and suggesting solutions.

   1   You go to bed late, so you have trouble waking up in the morning.

   2   You and two friends want to travel from Florida to Toronto together, but can't afford a flight.

   3   You only have 30 minutes for lunch, but there aren't any cafés or restaurants nearby.

   4   Your city has a growing number of homeless people and no money to house them.

2   Work in groups. Look at the poorly designed objects. Use language from the box to describe or identify the problems. Then suggest one or more solutions.

1

2

3

Pronunciation for speaking

Using intonation to make declarative statements

Statements, i.e. sentences that give facts, or information, as opposed to questions, or commands, typically have a "2–3–1" intonation pattern in English. This means the speaker's voice begins on level 2 ("neutral"), jumps up to 3 ("high") on the last stressed syllable, and then steps down to 1 ("low"). There are two specific rules concerning the pronunciation of declarative statements:

1 If the last stressed syllable is also the last syllable, the speaker's voice jumps up to 3, and then glides down to 1 on that syllable:

It's a poorly designed **door**.

2 If the last stressed syllable is before the last syllable, the voice jumps up to 3 on that syllable, and then steps down to 1:

She didn't understand the ass**ign**ment.

1 **2.4 Listen to the declarative statements. Notice the last stressed syllable. Draw the intonation contours according to the rules in the box above.**

1 The instructions weren't clear.

2 Don Norman is an American designer.

3 The kitchen has a lot of fancy tools.

4 Virtual reality is used to train surgeons.

5 Arachnophobia is a fear of spiders.

6 Someday soon there may be augmented cooking lessons.

2 **Work with a partner. Choose the last stressed syllable of each statement. Draw the intonation contour. Then practice saying the statement.**

1 I have a real problem with umbrellas.

2 Plastic is flexible.

3 The product is environmentally friendly.

4 I have an idea.

Speaking task

Design and present a new product that solves a problem.

Brainstorm

In groups, make a list of problems or needs you have encountered in your everyday life or in an area such as the ones below.

education	health	entertainment	fashion	communication
business	sports	science	media	engineering

Plan

Design a product to solve one of the problems you listed in the Brainstorm step. It can be an object, a service, or an AR or VR program. As much as possible, your design should match the criteria for good design. Use drawings or models to help you understand the problem. Don't criticize, but work together to come up with more new ideas.

Speak

Practice your presentation. Try to answer the following questions in your presentation.

What is the problem?

What are the weaknesses of existing solutions?

What is your new product, and how will it solve the problem?

Share

Present your product to the class. Speak for two minutes.

Reflect

Work with a partner. Discuss the questions.

1 How does a well-designed product make our lives easier? In contrast, how does a poorly designed product create problems for us? Give examples.

2 Would you enjoy having a career as a designer? Why? / Why not?

Review

Wordlist

MACMILLAN
DICTIONARY

Vocabulary preview

artificial (adj) **	device (n) ***	functional (adj) **	similarity (n) **
come up with (phr v)	feature (n) ***	layer (v) ***	simulation (n) *
complex (adj) ***	feedback (n) **	measure (v) ***	three-dimensional (adj)
computer-generated (adj)	figure out (phr v)	operate (v) ***	train (v) ***

Vocabulary development

classic (adj) **	environmentally friendly (adj)	image (n) ***	measurement (n) **
element (n) ***	flexible (adj) **	industrial (adj) ***	process (n) ***

Academic words

alter (v) **	eventually (adv) ***	interact (v) *
contrast (n) ***	income (n) ***	substitute (n) *

Academic words review

Complete the sentences using words from the box.

altered   eventually   income   structure   substitute

1   In most recipes, milk can be used as a _____ for cream.

2   The company hasn't significantly _____ its approach since the 1980s.

3   After an eight-hour climb, the group _____ reached the summit.

4   The Metropol Parasol in Seville, Spain, is a unique _____. It is the largest timber-framed building in the world.

5   In the Gulf States people don't have to pay _____ tax on their earnings.

Unit review

Listening 1		I can infer meaning from context.
Listening 2		I can listen for key terms and definitions.
Study skill		I can be creative when problem solving.
Vocabulary		I can use design vocabulary.
Grammar		I can use *wish* when referring to present or future time.
Speaking		I can talk about problems and solutions.

Discussion point

Discuss with a partner.

1 Why do you think Millennials are more forgetful than their parents?

2 Which of these facts surprised you the most?

3 What other "amazing facts" do you know about the human brain?

GLOSSARY

meditation (n) the act of thinking calmly for a long period to help you relax

multitasking (n) the activity of doing more than one thing at the same time (e.g. talking on the phone while working on the computer)

Your amazing brain

The **size** of your brain is not related to your intelligence. Einstein's brain was smaller than average!

Each time you have a new thought, a new connection is made between the cells of your brain.

Because of multitasking and lack of sleep, Millennials (people aged 18 to 34) are **more forgetful** than their parents.

On average, people have **70,000 thoughts** per day.

Your brain has enough memory to store **three million hours** of television.

The hippocampus—the part of the brain involved in processing emotions—is **larger** in women than in men.

Naps, meditation, and taking walks make your brain **more productive**.

New cells are born in the brain throughout a person's life. **You're never too old to learn!**

The same part of the brain processes **physical** and **mental** pain. That's why a "broken heart" hurts!

VIDEO

WORLD MEMORY CHAMPIONSHIPS

Before you watch

Predict which numbers complete each sentence, then watch the video and check.

three   six   eight   nine

1 The World Memory Championship takes place over _____ days.

2 People from the age of _____ to 74 years participate.

3 Wang Feng prepares the championship for five to _____ hours a day.

4 Dominic O'Brien has won the championship _____ times.

UNIT AIMS

LISTENING 1 Understanding the structure of a formal argument
LISTENING 2 Listening for repair and elaboration
STUDY SKILL Organization and memory

VOCABULARY Words to describe the brain and mind
GRAMMAR Concession
SPEAKING Responding to an argument

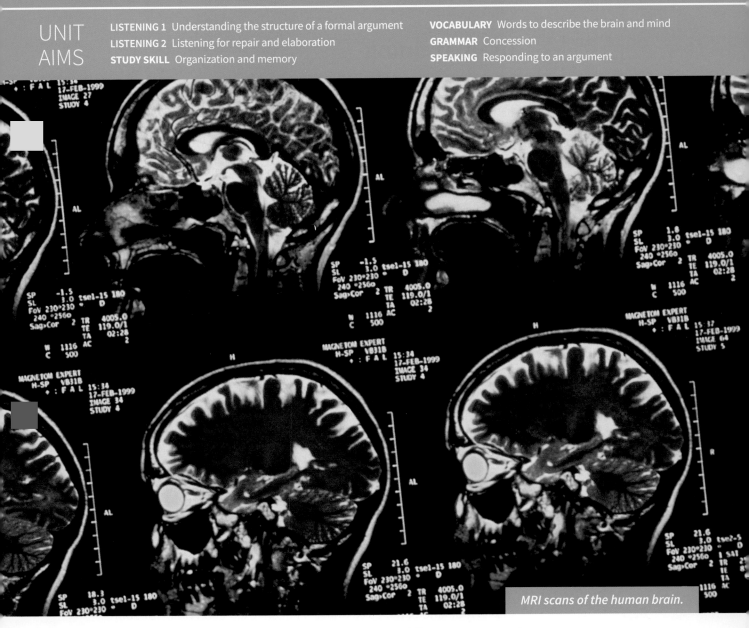

MRI scans of the human brain.

While you watch

Watch the video again and choose *T* (True) or *F* (False).

1   The World Memory Championships is a
    nine-day competition.   T / F

2   Wang Feng set a new world record for
    remembering names.   T / F

3   Dominic O'Brien says brain training helps
    with creativity.   T / F

4   Tony Buzan says your memory needs
    imagination to work well.   T / F

After you watch

Work with a partner. Discuss the questions.

1   Are you better at memorizing numbers, faces,
    or names? Why?

2   Which techniques do you use for remembering
    new vocabulary?

3   Two different pieces of advice for improving
    your memory were given in the video:
    practicing every day, and being creative and
    happy. Which do you think works better and
    why?

Brain training

A Vocabulary preview

1   Match the words in bold with the correct definitions.

1   The study explores the **claim** that Internet use damages people's memory.
2   Major changes in brain **function** occur during the teenage years.
3   The conclusions are based on a **sample** of over 1,000 volunteers.
4   Test subjects were given just five minutes to complete a memory **task**.
5   **Evidence** suggests that multitasking is actually inefficient.
6   I think all advertising companies are **dishonest**.
7   We didn't buy the toy because of **criticism** that it was not safe for children.
8   Many people believe that some apps have the **potential** to make them smarter.

a   (n) something that needs to be done
b   (n) a statement that something is true, even though you have not proved it
c   (n) a process that happens inside the body, or something that part of the body does
d   (n) a group of people who participate in a study or experiment
e   (n) facts or signs used to help prove something
f   (n) comments that show you think something is bad or wrong
g   (n) the possibility to develop or achieve something in the future
h   (adj) not truthful

2   Work with a partner. Discuss the questions.

1   Do you believe claims that exercise can improve your memory? Why? / Why not?
2   What kind of things can have a negative effect on brain function?
3   Are you good at multitasking (i.e. doing several tasks at the same time)?
4   There is evidence to suggest that use of mobile technology has a negative effect on our memory. Do you think this is true? Why? / Why not?
5   Are you good at receiving criticism? Why? / Why not?
6   Are ten people a big enough sample size for a scientific test? Why? / Why not?
7   Why would someone make a dishonest claim?
8   What are some of the potential benefits of artificial intelligence?

GLOSSARY

anecdotal (adj) based on someone's personal experience, rather than facts that can be checked

neuroscience (n) the scientific study of the brain and nerves in the body that control feelings

B Before you listen

Work with a partner. Discuss the questions.

1 What activities can make our brains work faster or more efficiently?

2 Do you think brain-training apps and games can make people more intelligent? Why? / Why not?

3 What experience do you have with these types of apps and games?

C Global listening

3.1 Listen to *Brain training* and choose the best option to complete the sentences.

1 Steve doesn't think there is any evidence that …

  a brain-training apps make you more intelligent.

  b brain-training apps make you better at games.

  c brain-training apps help you master new concepts.

2 Anna believes there is a lot of research to support …

  a a link between brain-training apps and improved focus.

  b a link between brain-training apps and improved brain function.

  c a link between brain-training apps and improved memory.

3 Anna and Steve agree that brain-training apps …

  a don't deliver what they promise.

  b aren't as effective as physical exercise.

  c have the potential to make you more intelligent.

4 The conversation is about …

  a claims made in brain-training advertisements.

  b problems with scientific research on brain training.

  c whether brain-training apps improve brain function.

D Close listening

Understanding the structure of a formal argument

In formal discussions and debates, speakers try to persuade listeners to agree with their point of view by presenting a **formal argument.** Formal arguments consist of two parts—a claim and supporting evidence.

A claim is the speaker's main idea or opinion. Phrases that signal a claim include:

I'm (not) convinced that… / I'd argue that… / My position is that…

All claims should be supported by **evidence** such as references to scientific research, statistics, or quotations from experts.

1 🎧 3.1 Listen to *Brain training* again. Write *Steve* or *Anna* next to the claim they make.

 1 There were issues with the brain-training research that showed positive results. _____

 2 A large group of scientists claims brain training does work. _____

 3 Most of the studies showing positive results were poorly designed. _____

 4 Brain training has the potential to make our brains work better. _____

 5 It's dishonest to sell brain-training apps that don't work. _____

2 🎧 3.1 Listen again. Match the supporting evidence (a–f) with the claims made in Exercise 1 (1–5).

 a Some studies compared brain-training apps with watching DVDs. ___

 b Companies marketing the apps earn over $25 million dollars a year. ___

 c Improvement doesn't seem to transfer into the real world. ___

 d 132 studies showed brain training can improve brain function. ___

 e Some of the best scientists in the world are working to develop tasks that make people smarter. ___

E Critical thinking

In a group, discuss who you think "won" the discussion, Steve or Anna. Explain your reasoning.

Study skills   Organization and memory

1   Read List A for 15 seconds, then cover it.
2   Say the words of a song to stop yourself practicing the list.
3   Write down the words you remember.
4   Check List A and note down your score.
5   Now do the same with List B.

List A

grandma   broccoli   fact   pants   coat
mail   number   mushrooms   gloves   kid

List B

VEGETABLE	PERSON	CLOTHING	MISC.
green beans	kid	coat	fact
mushrooms	uncle	pants	number
broccoli	grandma	gloves	mail

You probably remembered more items from List B, because:

(1) grouping similar items helps us remember.

(2) seeing that there are only four types of information makes the task manageable.

(3) the lists were nearly the same, and going over them again helps us remember them.

© Stella Cottrell (2013)

1   Work with a partner.

Student A: Write down 15 words you can think of which are foods, cities, or colors. Organize them into categories.

Student B: Write down words you can think of which are countries, animals, or school subjects. Make sure they are in a random order.

Swap lists. Read each other's list for 15 seconds, then try to write down as many words as you can remember. Who remembered the most?

2   Work with a partner. Discuss the questions.

1   How do you organize new language in your notebook?

2   What is the best way to remember new vocabulary?

Digital memory loss

A Vocabulary preview

1   Match the words in bold with the correct definitions.

   1   Listening to music doesn't **affect** my ability to concentrate while studying.

   2   I don't think using mobile devices has a significant **impact** on my memory.

   3   I can work more **efficiently** if I turn off my cell phone while studying.

   4   I think **capacity** is the most important thing to consider when buying a computer.

   5   In my opinion, a good memory is the most important **characteristic** of a good student.

   6   I write several **versions** of my essays before I hand them in to my professor.

   7   In my country, schools emphasize **critical thinking** more than memorization of facts.

   8   When I am working, I don't allow anything to **interfere** with my concentration.

   a   (n) amount of something that can be stored, e.g. on a computer or in the brain

   b   (n) an effect or influence on something

   c   (v) to disturb, prevent something from happening

   d   (v) to change or influence something

   e   (n) the ability to analyze and evaluate information without allowing emotions to influence you

   f   (adv) in a good way that doesn't waste time or energy

   g   (n) later, corrected, or changed forms of an original document, story, etc.

   h   (n) quality or feature that is a typical part of someone or something

2   Work with a partner. Which of the sentences in Exercise 1 are true for you?

B Before you listen

Activating prior knowledge

Work with a partner. Discuss the questions.

1   Does modern technology have a positive or negative effect on our memory?

2   Do you think people today need to remember as much as they did in the past?

3   What do you think is the difference between "short-term memory" and "long-term memory"?

C Global listening

1  **3.2** Listen to *Digital memory loss*. Number the topics in the order they're discussed.

___ How human memory works

___ Cognitive overload

___ Web design

___ How often we go online

___ Short-term and long-term memory

___ Habits to help the brain work efficiently

___ Hyperlinks

2 Choose the sentence that best expresses the speaker's main point.

1 There are two types of memory: short-term and long-term.

2 Research shows that hyperlinks harm students' ability to think critically.

3 The over-use of technology can harm the brain's ability to form and store memories.

4 Because of the Internet, people don't need to remember as many facts as they did in the past.

Listening for repair
and elaboration

D Close listening

In presentations and lectures, speakers sometimes make a mistake and need to correct what they've said. This is called a **repair**. To identify repairs, listen for signals like these:

Excuse me, what I meant to say was … / Let me rephrase that.

At other times, speakers may need to give examples, provide more detail, or explain something in a different way to make their ideas clearer. This is called **elaboration.** To identify elaborations, listen for signals like these:

To give an example … / To be more precise … / That is to say, … / In other words … / Basically, …

Listening for **repair** and **elaboration** will help you to identify specific details accurately.

 **3.2** Listen to *Digital memory loss* again. Choose *T* (True) or *F* (False).

1   73% of U.S. teens and 91% of adults go online every day.   T / F

2   Information is only briefly stored in short-term memory.   T / F

3   People can only remember 10 items for 7–15 seconds.   T / F

4   Turning off notifications when studying can improve memory.   T / F

E Critical thinking

Work in a group. Discuss the questions.

1   Compare the experience of reading online with reading printed text. How does the presence of hyperlinks change the way you read?

2   How do you predict people's ability to memorize information will change in the future?

Critical thinking

Appeal to popularity

Claiming that something is true because lots of people believe it is called an **appeal to popularity**. It is a flawed type of argument because in reality, it's possible for lots of people to believe something that isn't supported by facts or evidence. For example, many people used to believe that the Earth was flat – an idea later proven incorrect.

To properly evaluate an argument, we need to assess the evidence presented, not how popular something is.

1   🎧 **3.3** Listen to two extracts from *Brain training*. Decide whether the speakers make a valid argument or an appeal to popularity.

2   Work with a partner. Check (✓) the statements that illustrate an appeal to popularity.

   1 ☐ Companies that market brain games are earning more than $25 million a year for products that don't deliver what they promise. I think that's dishonest.

   2 ☐ Studies show that people of all ages perform more poorly on cognitive tests when they multitask.

   3 ☐ In one survey, 95% of college students reported reading assigned texts and watching television at the same time. I believe this proves that multitasking is not harmful.

   4 ☐ The new SmartPhone 5 is the best cell phone on the market today, as shown by the fact that more than 20 million people have bought it since it came out in 2016.

   5 ☐ Surveys show that 21% of adults, and 24% of teens are connected to the Internet almost constantly. Scientists are very interested in finding out what effect all this Internet use is having on people's brains.

3   Work in a group. Discuss the questions.

   1 Think of three examples when the majority of the population believed something that turned out to be false.

   2 Can you think of any examples of appeals to popularity in advertising? Why is this such a common strategy?

   3 What's the best way to respond to this type of argument in a discussion or debate?

Vocabulary development

Words to describe the brain and mind

1 Match the words in bold with the correct definitions.

1 Studies suggest that drinking water improves **concentration**.
2 Sharing can be a difficult **concept** for children to understand.
3 Stress has a negative impact on **short-term memory**.
4 According to the author Malcolm Gladwell, people need 10,000 hours of practice in order to **master** a skill.
5 **Mental** health issues can be difficult to identify.
6 I disagree with your **observation** that it's hard to read and listen to music at the same time.
7 Turning off my cell phone helps me to **focus** when I'm writing an academic paper.
8 Dr. Shapiro is a **psychologist** who specializes in the behavior of young children.

a (v) to pay close attention to something
b (v) to learn how to do something extremely well
c (adj) relating to the brain or mind
d (n) giving all of your attention to something
e (n) an idea, thought, or theory
f (n) a professional who studies how the mind affects human behavior
g (n) the ability to remember recent events or information for a short period of time
h (n) a comment about something seen or heard

2 Work with a partner. Discuss the questions.

1 What has a negative effect on your concentration when you're studying?
2 Is it hard for you to focus in a noisy room?
3 Which skills would you like to master?
4 Which foods do you think can improve people's short-term memory?
5 Which activities in your daily life require the most mental effort?
6 Why do you think it's become more common to seek help from psychologists these days?
7 How do you feel when a professor makes an observation about your coursework?
8 What is a concept you find difficult to understand?

Academic words

1 Match the words in bold with the correct definitions.

1 **contemporary** (adj)
2 **context** (n)
3 **contradict** (v)
4 **identify** (v)
5 **intelligence** (n)
6 **revenue** (n)

a to be so different from another piece of information, that both cannot be true

b the ability to understand things quickly and apply knowledge to a high level

c modern, relating to the present time

d to recognize something and understand exactly what it is

e the money generated by a business

f the general situation in which something happens

2 Complete the sentences with the words in bold from Exercise 1.

1 In general, digital technology has had a negative effect on _____ society.

2 Testing and exams are the best way to measure _____.

3 Cell phones should never be used in an educational _____.

4 Brain-training companies are more concerned about _____ than about making people smarter.

5 It's never acceptable to _____ your lecturer.

6 It's important to _____ potential weaknesses in your own arguments.

3 Work with a partner. Which of the sentences in Exercise 2 do you agree with? Why?

Speaking model

You are going to learn about concessions, responding to an argument, and word stress in statements of contradiction. You are then going to use these to hold a debate about the use of technology in education.

A Analyze

Read part of a debate and answer the questions below.

> **Evan:** Look, I think it's better to type notes with a laptop than to write everything by hand. For one thing, writing for a long time can be physically tiring. Typing on a laptop causes much less muscle strain. Secondly, typing is more efficient because most people can type much faster than they can write. As a result, students who type can write down almost every word the professor says. That way they can be sure not to miss anything.
>
> **Jay:** While I agree that typing is more comfortable than writing by hand, I think there's a problem with your second argument. It's true that typing enables us to write down almost everything the professor says, but that isn't necessarily a good thing because recording every word doesn't require us to interact with the information in ways that help us master it. In fact, a contemporary research paper on note-taking found that students who took notes by hand understood concepts better, and were able to apply them more successfully than students who typed notes on a computer or mobile device. The researchers' explanation was that because handwriting is slower and we can't write everything, we're forced to listen, think, and summarize the information, and this mental effort helps comprehension, and memory. In contrast, it's easy to type automatically, without processing the information. So, the fact that handwriting is slower turns out to be an advantage, while the fact that typing is faster is actually a disadvantage.

1 What is Evan's claim and what reasons does he provide to support it?

2 What is Jay's claim and what reasons does he provide to support it?

3 Which speaker did a better job of supporting their position, in your opinion?

B Discuss

Work with a partner. Discuss the questions.

1 Do you usually take lecture notes by hand, or on a device such as a laptop or tablet? Why?

2 After this class, will you change your method of taking lecture notes? How?

3 Is it possible to use technology in ways that encourage interaction with information in order to remember it better? How?

Grammar

Concession

In discussions and debates you can make arguments more persuasive by agreeing with part of your opponent's position, then contrasting it with your own.

We use the following to make concessions:

Conjunctions	*Although* / *Even though* / *Though* tablets are useful, there is no evidence that they improve academic performance.
may / might + but	Using mobile devices **might** improve engagement, **but** there is nothing to suggest it improves performance.
Adverbials	Cell phones can affect concentration. **Nevertheless** / **Nonetheless**, they play an important role in modern education.

1 **Match the two halves to form sentences.**

1 While it's true that smartphones have made our lives easier,

2 Although brain-training apps can be fun to play,

3 That may be true,

4 Students enjoy using mobile devices in the classroom.

5 Even though many students prefer to take notes on their laptops,

a I don't believe they make you smarter.

b research suggests this actually has a negative effect on their understanding of the subject.

c but modern students expect to use technology in the classroom.

d they have had a negative impact on our memory.

e Nevertheless, research shows that the highest-performing schools in the world have lower levels of computer use.

2 **Rewrite the sentences using the words in parentheses.**

1 Students enjoy using mobile devices in the classroom. Studies show this has a negative effect on exam performance. (although)

2 Some students are easily distracted by the Internet. Others find it a useful research tool. (while)

3 Modern websites are more interesting. They actually have a negative effect on our memory. (may / but)

4 Technology can have a powerful impact on learning. Most teachers think cell phones are a distraction in class. (Nevertheless)

5 Students say technology has improved their education. Much more research is needed to prove this is true. (Even though)

Speaking skill

A key part of speaking in a debate is responding to your opponent's claims and arguments. There are three common ways to do this:

1 Point out the weakness of your opponent's evidence, sources, or logic.

Those studies were poorly designed. There's no evidence to support that claim.

2 State an opposing claim or opposing argument and provide evidence to support it.

I think the opposite is true. According to [source], …

I disagree. Research shows …

3 Concede your opponent's point is partly correct, then contrast it with your own.

You may have a point there, but …   That may be true, but …

1 🎧 3.4 Listen to five short dialogues and complete the sentences.

1 A: A professor at Stanford University, Clifford Nass, says that listening to music with words can interfere with a person's ability to focus on reading and writing tasks.

B: _____, lots of studies have shown that listening to classical music can help boost concentration.

2 A: I think students take better lecture notes when they use a laptop instead of writing by hand.

B: _____ to support that idea. In fact, the sources I've read say that students remember information better if they take notes by hand.

3 A: Online courses are super-convenient, don't you agree?

B: _____, but I think face-to-face courses are a lot more interesting.

4 A: This article says that lost or damaged brain cells aren't replaced in adults.

B: That research is way _____. Scientists have known for a long time that some parts of the brain can continue to produce new cells even into old age.

5 A: Kids are spending too much time playing games online. It's a waste of time.

B: _____. Studies have shown that online games can increase teamwork among children and promote creativity.

2 Work with a partner. Take turns responding to the statements below using techniques from the Speaking skill box.

1 Brain-training apps make you more intelligent.

2 Cell phones have a negative impact on our memories.

3 Laptops make it easier to take notes.

Pronunciation for speaking

> ## Stress in statements of contradiction
>
> In English, the last content word of a phrase, clause, or short sentence normally gets the strongest stress:
>
> *The professor spoke SOFTly.*   *I prefer taking notes by HAND.*
>
> However, a speaker may shift away from the basic stress pattern to **contradict** something a previous speaker has said:
>
> A: *I think multitasking is an efficient way to do several tasks at the same time.*
>
> B: *I disagree. There's lots of research proving that multitasking ISN'T efficient because it slows you down.*
>
> Note that in contradictions, speakers use *do / does / did* in affirmative statements:
>
> A: *The researchers didn't say that cell phones cause lower test results.*
>
> B: *Actually, they DID say that. They said there is a possible relationship between the two.*

1 🎧 **3.5 Listen to part of the conversation from *Brain training*. Complete the sentences with one word. Why does the speaker stress these words?**

   1 First of all, there's a pretty big group of researchers who claim brain training _____ work.

   2 One website published a list of 132 studies showing that brain training _____ improve brain function.

2 🎧 **3.6 Read the dialogues. Predict which word Speaker B will stress most strongly. Then listen to check your predictions.**

   1 A: These statistics aren't correct. The numbers are too large.

      B: They are correct. I reviewed them myself and I'm sure they're right.

   2 A: We don't need to remember numbers anymore because we can store them on our cell phones.

      B: I think we do need to remember them. What if you lose your cell phone?

   3 A: Taking notes by hand is inefficient because we can't write everything.

      B: Researchers say that's a good thing because it forces you to think about what you choose to write.

   4 A: It's not good for young children to learn two languages at the same time. It confuses them.

      B: It doesn't confuse them. In fact, it makes them smarter!

Speaking task

Debate the positive and negative effects of technology on academic performance.

Brainstorm

Work in groups of four. Discuss the effects of technology on education. Think about the following:

> access to information   potential for teaching outside the classroom
> dependency on technology   effects on our memory
> use of media in the classroom   collaboration

Plan

Divide each group into two pairs.

Pair 1: Present the positive effects of technology on academic performance.

Pair 2: Present the negative effects of technology on academic performance.

With your partner, plan for the debate by following these steps:

1   Choose the three best arguments from the brainstorming session to support your position.

2   Find evidence (e.g. reasons, facts, expert quotations, findings from research, etc.) to support each argument.

3   Try to predict the opposing team's arguments. Decide how you will respond: by conceding, or by presenting counter-arguments.

Speak

Get back into groups of four and hold your debate. After each argument is presented, allow time for concession or counter-arguments. Use concession language from page 57 and remember to use the correct intonation when contrasting ideas.

Share

Work as a class to discuss the result of the debates. Choose one member of your group to summarize the main points presented in your debate. Compare ideas.

Reflect

Work with a partner. Discuss the questions.

1   Does technology have a positive or negative effect on your studies?

2   How will you try to change your "technology habits" in the future?

Review

Wordlist

MACMILLAN DICTIONARY

Vocabulary preview

affect (v) ***	critical thinking (n)	evidence (n) ***	potential (adj) ***
capacity (n) ***	criticism (n) ***	function (n) ***	sample (n) ***
characteristic (n) **	dishonest (adj) *	impact (n) ***	task (n) ***
claim (n) ***	efficiently (adv)	interfere (v) **	version (n) ***

Vocabulary development

concentration (n) ***	focus (v) ***	mental (adj) ***	psychologist (n) **
concept (n) ***	master (v) *	observation (n) ***	short-term memory (n)

Academic words

contemporary (adj) ***	contradict (v) *	intelligence (n) **
context (n) ***	identify (v) ***	revenue (n) **

Academic words review

Complete the sentences using words from the box.

context	contradict	diverse	identify	interact

1 It took years of painstaking research to _____ the cause of the disease.

2 The findings seem to _____ earlier studies into teenage brain development.

3 It's important to be able to guess the meaning of new vocabulary from _____.

4 It is fascinating to watch young children playing and see how they _____ with one another.

5 The magazine covers a _____ range of issues.

Unit review

Listening 1	☐	I can understand the structure of a formal argument.
Listening 2	☐	I can listen for repair and elaboration.
Study skill	☐	I know about organization and memory.
Vocabulary	☐	I can use words to describe the brain and the mind.
Grammar	☐	I can use phrases to show concession.
Speaking	☐	I can respond to an argument.

Discussion point

Discuss with a partner.

1 What are five words you associate with "fire"? Are the words mostly positive, negative, or neutral?

2 When was the last time you were near a fire? Why do you remember it?

3 What are some ways fire can be used to benefit us?

Uses *of* fire

Cooking and heating[1]

About three billion people worldwide cook and heat their homes with fire.

Lighting

Candles are used in seven out of ten households in the U.S.

Ceremonies

The Oniyo New Year's Fire Festival in Japan has been celebrated for the past 1,600 years.

Manufacturing

Fire is used in the production of 1,600 metric tons of steel every year.

VIDEO

CHILEAN FOREST FIRES

Before you watch

Match the words in bold with the correct definitions.

1 **agricultural** (adj)   a planned or done deliberately

2 **harvest** (n)   b related to farming

3 **heatwave** (n)   c a unit for measuring land, equal to 10,000 square meters

4 **hectare** (n)

5 **intentionally** (adv)   d an unusually long period of very hot weather

e the activity of collecting a crop

UNIT AIMS

LISTENING 1 Listening to distinguish between fact and opinion
LISTENING 2 Listening for sequence of events
STUDY SKILL Reviewing notes

VOCABULARY Synonyms
GRAMMAR Using stance markers
SPEAKING Changing the topic and returning to it

A campfire in the desert.

While you watch

Watch the video and choose *T* (True) or *F* (False).

1 The fires burned for four days before spreading to agricultural land. T / F

2 Juana Canales thinks the 2010 earthquake was much worse. T / F

3 Susana Molina lost her house during the fires. T / F

4 Felipe Zuniga doesn't think it will be possible to save the harvest. T / F

5 We don't know if the fires were started intentionally. T / F

After you watch

Work with a partner. Discuss the questions.

1 How do you think people accidentally cause forest fires?

2 What can you do to help prevent forest fires?

3 Which extreme weather conditions does your country or region suffer from?

The discovery of fire

A Vocabulary preview

Read the sentences. Choose the correct definitions of the words in bold.

1 The people **adapted to** a new lifestyle after they moved to the city.
   a to change behavior to deal with a new situation
   b to finish the last part of

2 Researchers are trying to find out more about the lives of our **ancestors**.
   a people who live nearby
   b people related to us who lived long ago

3 Evan used to eat mostly fast food, but **expanded** his diet to include more vegetables.
   a to make something smaller   b to make something larger

4 We **take it for granted** that we can use fire in daily life.
   a to accept without question   b to consider carefully

5 The forest fire grew quickly and **thus** caused a lot of damage.
   a in place of   b as a result

6 Fires can provide **protection** at night from wild animals.
   a danger   b safety

7 Cooking meat helped to **preserve** it, and so it lasted longer.
   a keep something from decaying   b improve the taste of something

8 Fires provide people with **warmth** on cold nights.
   a the light provided by something   b the heat produced by something

B Before you listen

Activating prior knowledge

Work with a partner. Discuss the questions.

There was a time in the past when people didn't use fire. What do you think life was like then? Think about:

what people ate	what people did to socialize
what people made	where people lived

C Global listening

🎧 **4.1** Listen to *The discovery of fire*. Then answer the questions.

1   What is the discussion mainly about?
   a   A comparison between types of food.
   b   Why our ancestors' lives changed.
   c   How scientists gather evidence.

2   In the discussion, "the controlled use of fire" is defined as:
   a   a discovery made 4,000 years ago.
   b   using fire carefully in situations.
   c   using fire to benefit daily life.

3   What is described as a "major turning point" for our ancestors?
   a   using fire for protection
   b   using fire to cook food
   c   using fire to see at night

4   The main benefit mentioned of cooking food was:
   a   people hunted more.
   b   people lived longer.
   c   people enjoyed it.

5   According to researchers, why is the use of fire an application of technology?
   a   It was used to improve life.
   b   It was a major change.
   c   It was something new.

D Close listening

In lectures, presentations, and discussions speakers use a combination of **facts** and **opinions** to present their ideas.

Facts are statements that are known to be true or can be proved. Listen for the following signals to identify facts:

Scientists have **demonstrated** *that ...*   ***According*** *to research by ...*

These findings **confirm** *that ...*   *Scientists have recently* **discovered** *that ...*

Opinions are someone's thoughts or beliefs. Listen for the following signals to identify opinions:

Researchers claim that ...   *Scientists argue that ... Some consider ....*

In my view ...   It seems that ... Many people suggest that ...

Distinguishing between facts and opinions will help you better evaluate the ideas and arguments being presented.

1   🎧 **4.1** Listen to *The discovery of fire* again and complete each sentence with no more than two words.

   1   _____ research, no one is absolutely certain when fire was first used regularly.

   2   From what I've found, it _____ that the discovery of the controlled use of fire dramatically changed the lives of our ancestors.

   3   Findings _____ people started to live in colder climates than they could before without a source of heat.

   4   In _____, by building fires at night, our ancestors could greatly improve their own comfort and safety.

   5   Cooked food, _____, was a major turning point for our ancestors.

   6   Their _____ that as our ancestors adapted to eating a wider range of food, they were healthier and able to survive longer.

   7   I read that some researchers _____ using fire a step forward in our use of technology.

2   **Work with a partner. Discuss the questions.**

   1   Are the sentences in Exercise 1 facts or opinions?

   2   What other details did you hear that support the ideas in Exercise 1?

E Critical thinking

In a group, discuss what you think the speaker meant when they said that using fire was a "turning point" in history. What are some other turning points in human history?

Study skills | Reviewing notes

What does revision involve?

- *Organising your notes* – the process of sorting out what is 'essential' helps to remind you of material covered.

- *Reduce your notes* – to key headings, points and citations (name and date only).

- *Make master cards* – using memory triggers. You could also use pattern notes or concept pyramids.

- *Check your learning*. Write and test recall of difficult material several times to build your memory.

© Stella Cottrell (2013)

1 Work in a group. Discuss what Aida is doing right / wrong when reviewing her notes.

> Aida is a busy second-year student. She attends six lectures a week. She has many pages to read in her textbooks every night. Every night at home, she quickly reads over her notes. On the weekends, she studies alone. Sometimes, she goes to the library where she reviews her notes by herself. If she sees a note that is unclear, she writes *?* next to it, but she doesn't usually take time to ask someone for help, or to look up the information in her textbook. Before exams, she goes over her notes, but her notes often aren't clear enough to help her prepare well for her exams. She often doesn't do as well on her exams as she would like to.

2 Look at these suggestions for reviewing notes. Work with a partner and discuss the advantages of each.

1 Read through your notes. Write *?* next to anything that is unclear.

2 After the lecture, compare your notes against your textbook to see if any details are missing.

3 Find a classmate to review notes together. Use your notes to discuss the main ideas in your own words. Help each other to understand parts that are unclear to either of you.

4 Add to your notes or make corrections as you review them.

5 Ask yourself: what do I understand? What do I need to get more information about?

6 Rewrite your notes to make them clear to you later, and to help you recall the information that you have reviewed.

Forest fires: friend or foe?

A Vocabulary preview

1 Match the words in bold with the correct definitions.

1 The forest fire was the largest **natural disaster** in the country's history.
2 The fire was started **accidentally** when a man dropped his cigarette.
3 The **destruction** caused by the fire was shocking.
4 When a fire **breaks out**, the first response is to put it out.
5 When the wind blew, it **spread** the seeds of the plant.
6 Removing dead trees **lowers** the risk of a big fire.
7 The **inner** part of the tree was alive, but the outer part looked dead.
8 Lightning strikes **cause** around 10% of forest fires in the U.S.

a (v) to reduce something in strength, amount, degree
b (n) an event in nature that kills or injures a lot of people
c (n) the damage caused to something such that it can't be used again
d (adj) on the inside of something
e (v) to make something happen
f (adv) by mistake, not on purpose
g (v) to start suddenly (usually a fire, war, or disease)
h (v) to move something so it covers a large area

2 Complete the sentences with words from Exercise 1. Change the form if necessary.

1 If a fire starts to _____, the situation can quickly become dangerous.
2 Forest fires have _____ across the southeastern US.
3 Locals were shocked by the _____ to public property in the area.
4 The 2011 tsunami was one of the worst _____ in recent history.
5 The _____ city was largely unaffected by the storm.
6 They were given six months' detention for _____ starting the fire.
7 The tsunami was _____ by a huge earthquake off the coast.
8 Rain _____ the risk of forest fires.

B Before you listen

Activating prior knowledge

Work with a partner. Discuss the questions.

1 Fire is sometimes called a foe. A foe is an enemy. How would you define an enemy?
2 Fire is also sometimes called a friend. What are the characteristics of a friend?
3 Why might fire be considered both a foe and a friend?

C Global listening

🎧 **4.2** Listen to *Forest fires: friend or foe?* and check (✓) the topics mentioned.

- [ ] the main reason a forest fire is called a "foe"
- [ ] a scientific description of what a fire needs to burn
- [ ] some causes of forest fires
- [ ] the usual response to a forest fire
- [ ] regions in the world with the most fires
- [ ] the factors that make fires spread
- [ ] several benefits of a forest fire
- [ ] the process of a new forest growing after a fire

Listening to understand
a sequence of events

D Close listening

A sequence is a series of related events that happen in a specific order.

The following words and phrases are used to describe the order of events:
first, second, third, then, next, later, after / before that, after that happens, afterward, eventually, finally, last.

Note that sometimes a speaker doesn't present events in the order they actually happened. Therefore, it's important to pay attention to these signal words to help you keep track of the correct sequence.

1   🔊 4.2 Read the sentences. Then listen to *Forest fires: friend or foe?* again and decide if the sequences described are correct or incorrect.

1   If someone drops a burning cigarette, a fire burns out of control, and then spreads.

2   A fire clears away dead trees and plants, then new plants can grow.

3   When the banksia bush burns it releases seeds. Then its cones open.

4   After a fire starts, the blue beetle senses the fire, flies into the burning area, and lays its eggs while the fire is burning. Eventually the eggs are burned by fire in the trees.

5   After a fire, the ecosystem is restored because first the fast-growing plants start to grow, then the trees, and finally the slower-growing plants.

2   Work with a partner to make the sequences correct. Add any other details you can remember.

E Critical thinking

Work in a group. Discuss the questions.

1   Should forest fires be put out quickly or allowed to burn? Discuss the pros and cons.

2   What are possible long-term benefits of other natural disasters?

Critical thinking

Distinguishing between causation and correlation

Causation and correlation are both terms used to describe relationships between events. However, their meaning is different.

Causation describes the relationship between cause and effect (**A** causes **B**):

A _huge forest fire_ broke out and _destroyed over 1,200 homes in the area_.

   (*A* = cause)   >   (*B* = effect)

Correlation describes a relationship between two things that change at the same time. For example:

Between 1996 and 2010, sales of lemons in the U.S. increased, while the number of car accidents decreased.

The two events are correlated because they happened at the same time, but this doesn't mean that one *caused* the other. There is no evidence to suggest that increased sales of lemons *caused* fewer people to crash their cars. It's more likely that the events are unrelated.

However, often there is a third factor that explains the correlation:

Sales of ice cream and shark attacks both increase during the summer.

These events are correlated, but there is no evidence to suggest that ice cream sales *cause* shark attacks. It's more likely that people buy more ice cream in the summer because it's hot. They also go to the beach more, which makes it more likely they will be attacked by a shark.

1   🎧 **4.3** Listen to part of *Forest fires: friend or foe?* again. Answer the questions.

   1   Have forest fires in the U.S. increased or decreased since the 70s and 80s? By how much?

   2   How has the climate changed where the fires are?

   3   Do these factors make it more or less likely that forest fires will break out?

2   Work with a partner. Read the examples of correlation below and discuss what third factor might have caused both things to change.

   1   Forest fires and sales of sunglasses both increase at the same time.

   2   The more cafés there are in a place, the higher the crime rate.

   3   The more you weigh, the bigger your vocabulary is.

   4   Students who pay for extra math classes often get lower test scores.

3   Work with a partner. Discuss the questions.

   1   In the U.S., new drugs are tested for up to 12 years to prove that they cause a positive effect. Why is this important?

   2   Why do newspapers often choose dramatic headlines like, *"Eating X causes cancer,"* rather than *"Eating X and cancer are correlated"*?

Vocabulary development

Synonyms

Synonyms are words that have the same or similar meanings.

*He used water to **extinguish** / **put out** the fire.*

*Climate change is causally **linked** / **tied** to increased numbers of forest fires.*

*This is a **complete** / **total** disaster!*

*Before the controlled use of fire, our ancestors ate **raw** / **uncooked** food.*

A synonym can also be a phrase or expression, especially in idiomatic speech.

to get burned	*to be on fire*	*to burn someone up*
to be fired up about something	*to be burned out*	

1 **Read each sentence. Circle the two synonyms of each word in bold.**

1 The controlled use of fire was a **turning point** in human history.
   a critical moment   b crossroads   c disaster

2 The controlled use of fire **dramatically** changed daily life in so many ways.
   a slightly   b substantially   c noticeably

3 Cooking gave people a lot more food **options** than in the past.
   a selections   b observations   c alternatives

4 Food could be **stored** and used later.
   a kept   b saved   c avoided

5 Do the benefits of a forest fire **justify** all the destruction?
   a rationalize   b contribute to   c excuse

6 People could **maintain** a better diet for themselves and be healthier.
   a to continue with   b to keep up   c to consider

2 **Replace the words in bold with a synonym from the box.**

burns me up   burned out   fired up   got burned   on fire

1 I **was cheated** at the market—these jeans are fake!

2 He always keeps me waiting when we go out. That **makes me really angry**!

3 He's really **excited** about playing on Saturday.

4 Yousef is **unstoppable** – that's his fourth 3-pointer in a row.

5 Lack of motivation could be a sign you're **exhausted**.

Academic words

1 Match the words in bold with the correct definitions.

1 Sequoia trees **release** their seeds during forest fires.

2 U.S. researchers say CCTV cameras could help **detect** forest fires earlier.

3 Forest fires need three things to burn: fuel, oxygen, and a heat **source**.

4 The family worked hard to **restore** the house after it was damaged by fire.

5 After weeks of heavy rain in the area, new plants began to **emerge.**

6 The **sequence** of events that led to the fire remains unknown.

7 The smoke from the forest fire was **visible** for a long distance.

8 Firefighters **occupy** themselves between fires by watching TV.

a (v) to appear or become known

b (adj) that can be seen

c (v) to let something come out of a place it has been kept or trapped

d (v) to bring back a situation that was there before

e (v) to notice something, especially when it isn't obvious

f (n) the order that things happen or should happen

g (v) to fill your time or keep busy

h (n) where something comes from

2 Complete the sentences with words from Exercise 1. Change the form if necessary.

1 There are various devices you can buy to _____ smoke or fire in the household.

2 The sun is a _____ of heat for the Earth.

3 The city is raising money to _____ historic buildings following the fire.

4 Locals _____ themselves by clearing away the broken glass.

5 Even though the fire was out, the smoke from it was still _____.

6 Studies have _____ that suggest that 90% of forest fires are caused by humans.

7 The plants returned in _____ after the fire.

8 Fires _____ large amounts of CO_2 into the atmosphere.

3 Work with a partner. Discuss the questions.

1 Do you think it's important to restore historic buildings?

2 How do you occupy your time while waiting for a flight?

3 What steps would you take if you detected smoke in a building?

4 Describe the sequence of events leading up to an important event in your family or country's history.

Speaking model

You are going to learn about using stance markers and intonation to express feelings and attitudes, and phrases for changing a conversation topic and returning to it. You are then going to use these to hold an informal class debate about the ways fire is a positive and negative part of life.

A Analyze

Read the model and answer the questions below.

Yuki: Frankly, it's clear to me that there are so many benefits of using fire. For example, think about all the ways fire is used to manufacture the things we use. Fire is also used to cook and preserve food that we can buy at the store. Fires are a source of heat. They provide protection and warmth. I could go on about all the benefits.

Guy: Well, to be honest, I have to disagree with you. Let me explain why. According to the report we heard, fires can be natural disasters and cause a lot of destruction. Fire destroys homes and buildings. Fires can injure people.

Yuki: Speaking of injuries, that reminds me of another benefit. Fire is used in lots of ways in hospitals and in doctors' offices; for example, to make instruments sterile.

Guy: Yes of course you have a good point there but back to what I was talking about, fires do a lot of harm. Forest fires can release a lot of heat. They kill animals and plants. The smoke affects visibility. Birds have a hard time flying.

Yuki: As a matter of fact, while it's true that forest fires destroy a lot of trees every year, we also know that fires also help keep forests in balance.

Guy: As I was saying before, fires do a lot of harm, especially if they spread into towns and burn houses, and historic buildings. Houses can be replaced, but old, historic buildings can't.

Yuki: Sorry, but that reminds me of another benefit. Sometimes, when a fire spreads through a town, it can help the town get rid of old buildings it doesn't want. It might burn trash and old trees. Then, when the fire is gone, the town can make a fresh start. It's been cleaned up. Sounds good to me.

Guy: Anyway, I'm not sure it's as simple as that. Sometimes, no one detects a fire in time and many people are affected.

1 What is Yuki's attitude towards who will win the debate?
2 What phrase does Guy use to show disagreement with this opinion?
3 What phrases are used to change the topic?
4 What phrases are used to return to the topic?

B Discuss

With a partner, discuss which speaker you think presents the strongest position. Explain your reasoning.

Grammar

Using stance markers

Stance markers are used by speakers to express their attitude to the ideas they are presenting. They also help us know if an idea is an opinion or a fact. We can express stance with:

• single adverbs

Frankly, that seems like a huge benefit.

Actually, there are many benefits. For example, …

• adverbial clauses and prepositional phrases. In order not to sound impolite, support your stance with facts:

As a matter of fact, I didn't do the project alone. Hamid helped me.

To put it bluntly, I totally disagree with that idea. Let me explain why …

To be honest, that isn't really an example of how fire helps us. Consider this example …

1 🎧 4.4 Listen. For each conversation, choose an appropriate response.

1 a Frankly, it's too dangerous.　　b Actually, it's my favorite thing.

2 a Yeah, luckily it was late at night.　　b Actually, it's next week.

3 a To be honest, I thought it was boring.　　b Frankly, I'm not too worried.

4 a Actually, I don't want to go.　　b Actually, I don't like it.

2 Complete each conversation with a stance marker. More than one choice is possible. Practice with a partner.

1 A: That was an excellent restaurant. I'd definitely go there again.

  B: _____, I didn't like it at all. The service was awful.

2 A: You did great on the exam. You must have studied all weekend for it.

  B: _____, I spent over three weeks preparing for it. I knew it would be difficult.

3 A: I was worried I wouldn't be able to use this software, but _____, it's very easy to use.

  B: Yeah, I didn't have any problems with it either.

4 A: _____, I don't think it's a good idea to go away for the whole weekend.

  B: Well, then how about just going out for one of the days?

Speaking skill

Sometimes in a conversation, you may want to change the topic briefly. This often happens when someone says something that reminds you of something else.

Changing the topic

That reminds me. *Oh, by the way, …* *Speaking of …,*

Before I forget, I want to mention …

Returning to the topic

Back to what we were talking about … *Let's get back to …* *Anyway, …*

As I was saying before, …

During a debate in which you have limited time to present your ideas, try only to go off the main debate topic briefly, and then quickly return to it.

1 🎧 4.5 Listen and complete the sentences with the missing expressions.

1 OK, no problem. I'll meet you at the library at 7:30. _____, Mike was looking for you earlier.

2 You asked me about the lecture you missed. Oh, _____, we have an exam next Friday.

3 The first part of the lecture was clear. _____ talking about the last part. It was confusing.

4 You asked about my biology class. _____ classes, have you decided what to take next term?

5 Thanks for mentioning that article you found online. _____, does anyone know the answer to the second question?

6 _____, there are several benefits we need to consider.

2 Work with a partner. Use the framework to practice going off topic briefly then returning to it.

STUDENT A	STUDENT B
Tell your partner what you want to do after university. *I'm thinking about …*	Respond, then change the subject. *That sounds pretty interesting. By the way …*

STUDENT B	STUDENT A
Respond, then change the subject again. *That does sound like a good plan. That reminds me, …*	Respond, then change the subject back to your plans after university. *Oh, right. Anyway, as I was saying …*

Pronunciation for speaking

Using intonation to express feelings and attitudes

For someone to understand your ideas, they need not only to understand the words, but the feelings behind them. How quickly you say something, how your voice rises and falls, the tone and the pitch, all communicate your feelings and attitudes. By paying attention to your own intonation, you will make it easier for others to understand the ideas you want to communicate.

1 🎧 4.6 Listen to the same sentence said with three different intonations. Match the emotion with the sentence.

   1 I heard about a forest fire that happened recently. ___

   2 I heard about a forest fire that happened recently. ___

   3 I heard about a forest fire that happened recently. ___

   a excited   b afraid   c disinterested

2 Read each conversation. Decide what intonation will best communicate the ideas. Practice with a partner.

   1 A: There was a big fire not far from here yesterday.

       B: I know. I was totally scared it was going to spread this way.

       A: No kidding! We were lucky they were able to put it out so quickly.

   2 A: Do you want to hear some terrible news?

       B: What happened? Tell me!

       A: There was a big fire in the building where my sister lives. She lost everything.

       B: That IS terrible!

   3 A: Hey, look at this interesting chart about wildfires globally.

       B: Wow! I didn't know there were so many everywhere.

       A: Yeah, it's surprising how many fires there are annually!

Speaking task

Debate whether fire does more harm than good.

Brainstorm

Work in groups of four. Make a list of the many ways fire is part of life, both positive and negative.

In addition to what you learned in the unit, consider:

art	business	construction	manufacturing
natural disasters	medical treatment	emergencies	entertainment
injuries	trash removal		

Plan

1 Divide your group into two pairs.

   Pair 1: Discuss ways fire can be used to benefit our lives.

   Pair 2: Discuss ways fire can harm us.

2 With your partner, make a list of at least four ideas you plan to cover.

3 For each idea on your list, discuss the details you want to include with your partner. Take notes. Then decide who will present each idea in the debate. Consider the stance markers and what tone of voice will best express your feelings and attitudes. Review the phrases to use to go off topic and return to the topic.

Speak

Hold your debate. After each side presents, allow time for questions. Take brief notes on the other side's ideas.

Share

Work as a class to discuss the results of the debates. Choose one member of your group to summarize the main points presented in your debate. Compare ideas.

Reflect

Work with a partner. Discuss the questions.

1 Do you think the controlled use of fire is the biggest turning point in human history?

2 Do you think there will ever be a time where fire isn't used in society?

Review

Wordlist

MACMILLAN DICTIONARY

Vocabulary preview

accidentally (adv) *	cause (v) ***	lower (v) **	spread (v) ***
adapt to (v) **	destruction (n) **	natural disaster (n)	take something for granted (phr)
ancestor (n) **	expand (v) ***	preserve (v) ***	thus (adv) ***
break out (phr v)	inner (adj) ***	protection (n) ***	warmth (n) **

Vocabulary development

burn up (phr v)	fired up (phr v)	maintain (v) ***	turning point (n)
burned out (phr v)	get burned (phr)	option (n) ***	
dramatically (adv)	justify (v) **	store (v) ***	

Academic words

detect (v) **	occupy (v) ***	restore (v) ***	source (n) ***
emerge (v) ***	release (v) ***	sequence (n) ***	visible (adj) **

Academic words review

Complete the sentences using words from the box.

contemporary   detect   emerges   occupied   releases

1 The device can _____ small changes in temperature below the surface.

2 Burning fossil fuels _____ large amounts of CO_2 into the atmosphere.

3 Dubai Design District is a good place to visit if you want to see _____ design.

4 After several weeks, a butterfly _____ from the cocoon.

5 It's a good way to keep the children _____ for an hour or so.

Unit review

Listening 1		I can distinguish between fact and opinion.
Listening 2		I can listen for the sequence of events.
Study skill		I can review my notes.
Vocabulary		I can use synonyms of words.
Grammar		I can use stance markers.
Speaking		I can change the topic and return to it.

5 MOVEMENT

Supercommuters

INTERNATIONAL CITIES WITH THE LONGEST COMMUTES

Villavicencio, Colombia	3 hours 20 mins
Bangkok, Thailand	2 hours
Dubai, U.A.E.	1 hour 40 minutes
Lisbon, Portugal	1 hour 10 minutes
Manila, Philippines	50 minutes

AMERICAN CITIES WITH THE LONGEST COMMUTES

	Average commute time (in minutes)
New York, NY	35
Washington, D.C.	33.5
Boston, MA	31
Los Angeles, CA	28
California, CA	27

CHARACTERISTICS OF SUPERCOMMUTERS IN THE U.S.

- 70.5% drive alone
- Under 1% cycle to work
- 22.5% do some or all of their work at home
- Spend 130 mins commuting a week (average commute = 26 mins)
- Travel 82.5 miles one-way (average = 16.5) 16.5 miles

WHAT DOES COMMUTING DO TO YOUR HEALTH?

Commutes of ten miles or more can lead to…
- a rise in blood sugar, cholesterol, and blood pressure
- greater anxiety
- a decline in happiness and life satisfaction
- difficulty sleeping
- back ache.

Discussion point

Discuss with a partner.

1 Look at the list of cities with the longest single-journey commutes. What do you know about those places? Why do people spend so much time commuting?

2 What can people do to reduce the negative health effects of commuting?

3 What are some ways that people can make their commuting time more pleasant?

GLOSSARY

supercommuter (n) a person who travels more than 145 km (90 miles) one way to work

VIDEO

NEW YEAR IN THE CITY

Before you watch

Work with a partner. Discuss the questions.

1 How do you celebrate important events? Do you gather together with large groups of people?

2 How do you feel when you are in a large crowd of people?

3 How are large crowds of people controlled at a sports event or big celebration?

UNIT AIMS

LISTENING 1 Listening for generalized statements
LISTENING 2 Understanding priorities
STUDY SKILL Shortcuts in note-making: using abbreviations

VOCABULARY Compound adjectives
GRAMMAR Complex passives
SPEAKING Voicing and allaying concern

London commuters.

While you watch

Watch the video and answer the questions.

1 Where in the city is the event being held?

2 How many people gather here for New Year celebrations?

3 How many hours does Kim Austen still have to wait before midnight?

4 One of the overseas tourists traveled from Kyrgyzstan. Where is the other from?

5 What happens at midnight?

After you watch

Work with a partner. Discuss the questions.

1 How do you celebrate New Year's Eve in your city or country?

2 When you socialize, do you prefer meeting a small group of friends or being in a large crowd? Why?

3 Some people feel claustrophobic in a large group of people. What does this mean? How would you feel in a large crowd of people?

A very long commute

A Vocabulary preview

1 Read the sentences. Match the words in bold with the correct definitions.

   1 Winter flights may be cancelled due to **extreme** weather conditions.

   2 Working full-time and taking care of children can be **exhausting**.

   3 We had a seven-hour **layover**, so we decided to look around the city.

   4 Pollution is a **global** problem that needs to be addressed.

   5 Years of driving in **rush hour** no doubt contributed to Bob's high blood pressure.

   6 The area boasts **outstanding** transportation links.

   7 I believe children should be raised to have an independent **spirit**.

   8 Cycling is an **environmentally friendly** form of transportation.

   a (adj) excellent, great

   b (n) a short stay somewhere between two parts of a journey

   c (adj) very unusual or serious

   d (n) the time of day when roads are busy because lots of people are traveling to and from work

   e (n) one's attitude to life

   f (adj) designed not harm plants, animals, or the surroundings

   g (adj) making you feel very tired

   h (adj) relating to or including the whole world

2 Work with a partner. Discuss the questions.

   1 How does **extreme** crowding on trains or buses make you feel?

   2 What is the most **exhausting** part of your week? Why?

   3 Have you ever had a **layover** of more than seven hours? What did you do?

   4 What is the most important **global** issue we face?

   5 Would you accept a high-paying job even if it meant you had to drive in **rush-hour** traffic every day?

   6 Describe an **outstanding** concert or sports event that you have attended.

   7 Do you believe that listening to music is healthy for your **spirit**? What kind?

   8 What are the most / least **environmentally friendly** ways to commute?

B Before you listen

Activating prior knowledge

Work with a partner. Discuss the questions.

1 How long and how far would you be willing to commute to a job one-way?

2 "Mega" means "huge." How would you define a "mega-commute"?

C Global listening

🎧 **5.1** Listen to *A very long commute*. Choose the best answer for each question.

1   Where are the speakers?

    a   Silicon Valley   b   Mainz   c   Frankfurt

2   What do we learn about Carl?

    a   He's never been to Germany.

    b   He lives in San Francisco.

    c   He works in Silicon Valley.

3   Where will Andreas be for the next two weeks?

    a   Frankfurt   b   San Francisco   c   Mainz

4   What does Andreas find most difficult about his commute?

    a   the jet lag

    b   the physical difficulty

    c   the separation from his family

5   Why didn't Andreas move to the United States?

    a   Because his wife has a job in Mainz.

    b   Because his wife wants to be near her aging parents.

    c   Because his children do not speak English

6   In the United States, the average commute …

    a   is 26 minutes to work one-way.

    b   is 50 miles.

    c   takes about 15 minutes each way.

GLOSSARY

shuttle (n) a bus or train that travels regularly between two places, usually between an airport and the city center

D Close listening

1 🎧 **5.1** Listen to *A very long commute* again. Write *A* next to sentences that describe Andreas, and *C* next to sentences that describe Carl.

1 ____ teaches history at Pembroke State University.

2 ____ works for a company called M-Tech.

3 ____ commutes 16 hours to work.

4 ____ is married with children.

5 ____ thinks the lifestyle in the U.S. is too fast-paced.

6 ____ cycles to work every day.

Listening for
generalized statements

> A generalization is a statement that is true in most situations or for most people. To identify a generalization, listen for the following signal words and phrases:
>
> *In general, ... / Generally, ... / As a rule, ... / Most of the time, ... / Most ... /
> A majority of people ... / Normally, ... / Usually, ... / Typically, ... /
> An overwhelming number of people ...*

2 🎧 **5.2** Listen to extracts from *A very long commute* again. Choose *T* (True) or *F* (False), then correct the false statements.

1 Andreas generally gets a taxi to Frankfurt airport.	T / F
2 As a rule, Andreas flies nonstop from Frankfurt to San Francisco.	T / F
3 Andreas usually flies economy class.	T / F
4 Andreas generally has a problem with jet lag.	T / F
5 Carl's father normally leaves the house at 6:30 a.m.	T / F
6 Carl's commute generally takes 30 minutes each way.	T / F

E Critical thinking

Work in a group. Discuss the questions.

1 Why did Andreas and his wife decide not to move to the U.S.? Do you agree or disagree with their reasons?

2 Why do you think people choose to commute such long distances instead of finding work nearer where they live?

3 Would you ever commute so far to work? Why? / Why not?

Study skills | Shortcuts in note-making: use abbreviations

Abbreviations save time. Use them in your notes, but not in assignments.

- Work out a system you'll remember.
- Stick to your system.
- Introduce a few at a time, so that your notes make sense.
- Keep a "key" to your abbreviations to hand.

Useful common symbols and abbreviations

&(+)	and
+	in addition to
>	greater than / more than / better than
<	smaller / less than
→	this leads to / produces / causes
w/	with
e.g.	for example
i.e.	that is / that means
etc.	et cetera (and the rest)
NB	important
p.	page
para.	paragraph
ch.	chapter
C19	nineteenth century
Govt	government

© Stella Cottrell (2013)

1 Look at the list of common abbreviations above. What other abbreviations do you use? Discuss with a partner.

2 Play the game below with two partners. Was your text the same at the end?

Student A: Write a 4–5 line description of something you know a lot about, for example a process or specialist subject. Read it aloud to Student B.

Student B: Take notes using abbreviations from the box and your own. Then read your notes aloud to Student C.

Student C: Take notes using abbreviations from the box and your own. Then read your notes aloud to Student A.

Crowd management

A Vocabulary preview

1 Read the sentences. Match the words in bold with the correct definitions.

1 **barrier** (n)	a	the chance that something unpleasant or harmful could happen
2 **conventional** (adj)		
3 **emotional** (adj)	b	very interested in or excited by something
4 **enthusiastic** (adj)	c	to hurry or move quickly somewhere
5 **risk** (n)	d	the condition of being protected from danger or harm
6 **rush** (v)		
7 **safety** (n)	e	a type of fence that stops you entering a specific area
8 **venue** (n)	f	showing or making others show strong feelings
	g	usual, common, or accepted
	h	the place where an event happens

2 Complete the sentences with the words in bold from Exercise 1.

1 The show starts in 15 minutes, so we'd better _____ if we want to get good seats.

2 I'm not sure such a _____ approach will work here.

3 Allowing so many people onto the platform is a big _____.

4 The company hired extra security officers to maintain the _____ of the crowd.

5 Large groups of people are only dangerous if they become too _____.

6 Security cameras are installed throughout the _____.

7 Hundreds of _____ fans waited outside for their favorite singer to come out.

8 Fans broke through the _____ and ran onto the playing field.

B Before you listen

Activating prior knowledge

Work with a partner. Look at the picture on page 87 and answer the questions.

1 Where was this picture taken? What is happening?

2 What are some of the potential dangers of this situation?

3 What can event organizers do to prevent accidents in this situation?

C Global listening

🎧 **5.3** Listen to *Crowd management*. Choose the best answer for each question.

1 What is the seminar mainly about?

  a types of crowd

  b crowd safety

  c event planning

2 What type of crowd attends a sporting event?

  a a casual crowd

  b a conventional crowd

  c an expressive crowd

3 An acting crowd becomes dangerous when …

  a they wave signs.

  b they shout the names of their favorite players.

  c they rush onto the playing field.

4 Which of the following is *not* mentioned in connection with good planning?

  a The number of people attending the event.

  b Having state-of-the-art equipment.

  c Having good signage.

5 According to the speaker, why is it important to keep a crowd moving?

  a To stop people getting lost.

  b To prevent overcrowding.

  c To stop them rushing onto the playing field.

GLOSSARY

hazard (n) something that is dangerous

principle (n) a basic idea or rule that has a major influence on how something is done

sociology (n) the study of society and the way people behave towards each other

Understanding priorities

D Close listening

A priority is something important that must be done first, or that requires more attention than anything else.

The following expressions are often used to describe priorities:

Priority number one is …   *Our number one priority is …*

Our top priority is ….   *The most important thing to consider is …*

Our main concern is…

🎧 5.4 Listen to part 2 of *Crowd management* again and complete the notes with no more than three words.

PRIORITIES OF CROWD MANAGEMENT

General

Two main priorities:

1 = ¹_____*; prevent injuries + avoid accidents.*

2 = Make sure the event is ²_____.

Planning

Top priority = knowing the # of people ³_____.

Risk management

Identify ⁴_____ *(e.g. that hurt people / affect enjoyment) > Event organizer should reduce / correct risk.*

Communication

Priority = clear visual ⁵_____ *is key – stops people getting lost,*

⁶_____, *or injured.*

Crowd flow

Keep people ⁷_____ *to prevent* ⁸_____.

E Critical thinking

Work in a group. Discuss the questions.

1   What are some examples of casual and conventional crowds?

2   What can cause a crowd to become dangerously emotional?

3   What actions can you take to be safe at an outdoor venue such as a sports stadium?

Critical thinking

Slippery slope

Slippery slope arguments claim that allowing something relatively harmless today (event A) will start a trend that ultimately results in something terrible or extreme happening later (event Z). For example:

If we don't stop them raising fees this year,

soon we'll be paying $1 million dollars a semester!

      (event A)   >   (event Z)

This is illogical. There is no evidence that allowing the college to raise fees this year will ultimately lead to fees of $1 million a semester.

1 🎧 **5.5** Listen to a segment from *Crowd management*. Complete the slippery slope argument.

Fans wave a ¹_____ or ²_____ the name of their favorite team / player.
    People become emotional and jump out of their ³_____.
       A ⁴_____ occurs, with hundreds of people running down stairs, climbing over fences, etc.
          ⁵_____ can happen and people can get ⁶_____.

2 Work with a partner. Look at the slippery slope argument in Exercise 1 and answer the questions.

  1 What is the first event described?

  2 What is the extreme event described?

  3 Do you think the first event will necessarily lead to something so extreme?

3 Work in groups. Read the situations. Decide if they're reasonable arguments (e.g. the first event may well lead to the final event), or slippery slope arguments. Explain your answers.

  1 If we let children play video games every night, their grades will get worse and worse, and they won't be able to get a good job when they're older.

  2 Today you're ten minutes late, tomorrow it will be an hour. Before long you won't bother coming to work at all.

  3 John often downloads movies illegally. Pretty soon he'll be stealing from his parents or robbing banks!

Vocabulary development

Compound adjectives

A compound adjective is a single adjective formed from two or more words. Common types include:

compounds containing numbers
six-foot fence, *four-year* program

compounds containing -ed or -ing participles
far-reaching effects, *fast-moving* crowd, *ill-equipped* hospital

multiword compounds
state-of-the-art equipment, *up-to-date* plan

adjective + noun compounds
high-school student, *high-risk* situation, *last-minute* change

1   Complete the sentences with a compound adjective from the box.

> decision-making   high-priced   internationally recognized
> middle-class   slow-moving   three-bedroom   twelve-year-old

1   We were heartbroken when our _____ cat died.

2   The Fosters live in a _____ neighborhood, with many small homes and some apartments.

3   A _____ house is too small for a family with seven children.

4   The parking lot at the luxury hotel was crowded with _____ cars.

5   The committee's _____ process is slow and stressful.

6   The park is next to a _____ river.

7   The speaker is an _____ movie-maker.

2   Rewrite the sentences with a compound adjective.

1   Avi's commute lasts two hours.

   Avi has a _____ commute.

2   Why does Eva need a cell phone that costs three hundred dollars?

   Why does Eva need a _____ cell phone?

3   That is a good solution in the short term.

   That's a good _____ solution.

4   Normally, the class behaves extremely well.

   Normally it's an extremely _____ class.

5   English is spoken in several countries in east Africa.

   There are several _____ countries in east Africa.

Academic words

1 Choose the best definitions for the words in bold.

1 Our company has made a **commitment** to finish all repairs by the end of the summer.

    a promise   b request   c claim   d plan

2 It's important that the entrance has a strong **visual** impact.

    a relating to hearing   b relating to smell

    c relating to touch   d relating to sight

3 Once the program is approved, the city will need three years to **implement** it.

    a pay for it   b understand how to do it

    c stop it   d make it start to work

4 One **strategy** for managing people waiting in a queue is to provide them with entertainment.

    a clever trick   b bad idea

    c method for achieving something   d kind of force

5 The company uses CCTV cameras to **monitor** the behavior of customers throughout the store.

    a observe   b control   c change   d understand

6 If you include standing room, the stadium holds **approximately** 75,000 people.

    a close, but not exact   b exactly   c definitely   d comfortably

2 Work with a partner. Discuss the questions.

1 What kind of commitments to the public should venue owners make?

2 Is it important for signage to be visually appealing?

3 What kind of changes would you like to implement at your college or university?

4 Name three strategies for keeping people safe in a busy train station.

5 How do you feel if you know that cameras are monitoring you in a public place?

6 Approximately how long is your commute to college or university?

Speaking model

You are going to learn about complex passives, voicing concerns, and word stress in content and function words. You are then going to use these to assess and prioritize risks in a stadium and suggest solutions to each issue.

A Analyze

Work with a partner. Read the model and answer the questions below.

> **Alice:** Thank you, everyone, for completing the risk management checklists for the upcoming soccer game. It looks like you've identified seven potential problems. Let's try to prioritize them and work on finding solutions for each one.
>
> **Mark:** I'm a little concerned that there could be fights at the end of the game, like there were the last time these two teams played. Some people are bound to be upset if their team loses. So, I think preventing fights has to be our top priority.
>
> **Alice:** I agree that this is a major issue, which is why the board has recommended hiring five additional security teams.
>
> **Mark:** Good idea. At least one team should sit in each section of the stands, and additional teams should stand at the top and bottom of each staircase. If a fight breaks out, the teams can work together to pull people apart.

1 How many problems did the team identify in its risk assessment?

2 Which problem has top priority, according to Mark?

3 What solution does Alice propose?

B Discuss

Work with a partner. Discuss the questions.

1 Do you think Alice's suggestion will help to prevent fights?

2 What other steps can be taken to prevent fights from breaking out?

3 Have you ever attended an event where a fight broke out? How did the event organizers handle it? What did you do?

Grammar

Complex passives

The passive voice (*be* + past participle) can be used with all simple, continuous, and perfect tenses:

*The new seating area **will be installed** on Saturday.* (simple future)

*Previously, all maintenance **was being managed** externally.* (past continuous)

*Much of the signage on the first floor **has been replaced**.* (present perfect)

*Not all risks **had been** accounted for by the survey.* (past perfect)

We can also use the passive voice with modal verbs:

*Handrails **should** be installed throughout the venue.*

*All venues **must** be equipped with multiple emergency exits.*

Note we use the preposition *by* to introduce the agent:

*CCTV camera will be installed **by** CTFS on Monday.*

Remember to use prepositions that collocate with the past participle:

*The venue is comprised **of** five main seating areas.*

*All stands are equipped **with** safety barriers.*

1 Complete the sentences with the correct form of the verbs in the box.

damage	deal	discuss	injure	install	replace	report	spend

1 A large area of seating _____ in a fire last year.

2 More money must _____ on security around the venue.

3 This issue must _____ with immediately!

4 This section of the roof should _____. It's leaking.

5 Several cases of food poisoning _____ last year.

6 We're not sure yet. Lots of different options _____.

7 Better lighting _____ over the next few months.

8 Several people _____ by the time security arrived.

2 Rewrite these sentences with the correct form of the passive. Only include the agent if necessary.

1 They must install new lighting throughout the venue.

2 EAP has created a large new entrance on the south side of the stadium.

3 The board must address all potential hazards.

4 The company will replace all signage early next year.

5 The government has abandoned plans to update the health and safety guidelines.

Speaking skill

We can use the following phrases to express concern:

I'm concerned / worried that there aren't enough emergency exits.

I think / believe / fear the roof in this area might be a major / serious issue.

We have to make sure (that) this area doesn't get too crowded.

We can't have wet floors / broken turnstiles. That's really dangerous / unsafe.

Sometimes we need to make other people feel less worried or frightened about something. This is called **allaying concern**. To allay someone's concern we usually acknowledge the issue, and explain how we intend to solve it:

You're right—this area is poorly lit, which is why we're installing new lighting next month.

The lack of exits is being taken into account and we hope to have a solution by Friday.

1 🎧 5.6 Listen and complete the sentences with no more than two words.

1 A: I'm _____ there aren't enough emergency exits in this area.

   B: I agree that this is a major issue, and we will be discussing it in the next board meeting.

2 A: We _____ fire exits being blocked by unused sports equipment.

   B: Absolutely! All unused sports equipment will be removed by the end of the week.

3 A: We must _____ that there are enough security guards on game day.

   B: This is a top priority for us, which is why we have recruited 50 new security guards.

4 A: _____ overcrowding will be a big problem in this area.

   B: I agree, which is why a new entrance is being installed in the south stand.

5 A: I'm a _____ about the number of injuries on the stairs last year.

   B: We're concerned too, which is why we've asked for a full risk assessment of that area.

2 Work with a partner. Take turns allaying the concerns listed below.

1 I'm worried that the signage on the first floor is confusing.

2 We need to make sure that everyone understands the health and safety concerns.

3 I don't believe that there are enough parking spaces for this many people.

4 We can't have food being prepared so close to the toilet block.

Pronunciation for speaking

Word stress with content and function words

Words that convey meaning in English are called **content words**. They are normally stressed in sentences. Words that connect, replace, or show relationships are called **function words**. These are normally unstressed within sentences.

Content words	Function words
nouns (*crowd*, *risk*)	articles (*a*, *the*)
verbs (*rush*, *think*)	prepositions (*on*, *to*, *for*)
adjectives (*crowded*, *wet*)	pronouns (*you*, *them*)
adverbs (*very*, *extremely*)	conjunctions (*and*, *or*)
negatives (*not*, *never*)	be-verb (*is*, *are*)
demonstratives (*this*, *that*)	auxiliaries (*have*, *do*)

1 🎧 5.7 Listen and complete the sentences with the content words you hear. Then listen again and repeat.

1　I **think** the ＿＿＿＿＿＿ is the **biggest** ＿＿＿＿＿＿.

2　It's **dangerous** to have ＿＿＿＿＿＿ **floors** near the ＿＿＿＿＿＿.

3　I **don't think** there are ＿＿＿＿＿＿ ＿＿＿＿＿＿.

4　We **need** to ＿＿＿＿＿＿ a **handrail** on the ＿＿＿＿＿＿.

5　I'm ＿＿＿＿＿＿ about ＿＿＿＿＿＿ in the **east stand**.

2 🎧 5.8 Underline the words you think are stressed in each conversation. Then listen, check, and repeat.

1　A: We can't have wet floors in this area.

　　B: You're right, that's really dangerous.

2　A: The fence in this area isn't very strong.

　　B: That's true. Perhaps we should replace it.

3　A: Replacing the roof should be our top priority.

　　B: I agree. The old roof is a danger to fans.

4　A: The way to the toilets isn't well signposted.

　　B: I agree. It's confusing for fans.

5　A: There's only one exit for all fans.

　　B: Yes, that's a big problem.

Speaking task

You work for a risk assessment company. Assess and prioritize the risks to public safety in a stadium and suggest solutions to each issue.

Brainstorm

Work in groups of four. Discuss the potential risks in the stadium.

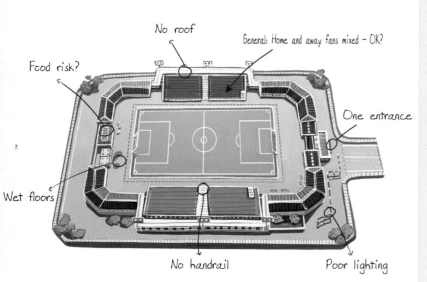

No roof

General: Home and away fans mixed – OK?

Food risk?

One entrance

Wet floors

No handrail

Poor lighting

Plan

Divide your group into two pairs.

Pair 1: Prioritize the risks you discussed and decide how to voice your concerns about each.

Pair 2: Think of solutions to the issues you discussed and decide how to allay concerns about each.

Speak

Work in the same groups.

Pair 1: Voice your concerns in order of priority, and discuss the proposed solutions.

Pair 2: Listen to each issue, and try to allay concerns by offering a solution.

Share

Work with another group. Explain the risks your group identified, and the solutions you agreed on. Use correct sentence stress as you present your ideas.

Reflect

Work with a partner. Discuss the questions.

1 Do you think more people will become super-commuters in the future, or will technology make it easier for people to stay and work in one place?

2 Why do you think people enjoy attending events like sporting events or concerts in large stadiums?

3 Have you ever attended an event in a large stadium? What was it? Do you think the event managers did a good job of controlling the crowd and managing risks?

Review

Wordlist

MACMILLAN
DICTIONARY

Vocabulary preview

barrier (n) **	exhausting (adj)	rush (v) **
conventional (adj) ***	extreme (adj) **	rush hour (n)
emotional (adj) ***	global (adj) ***	safety (n) ***
enthusiastic (adj) **	layover (n)	spirit (n) ***
environmentally friendly (adj)	outstanding (adj) **	venue (n) **
	risk (n) ***	

Vocabulary development

decision-making (adj) *	middle-class (adj) *	three-bedroom (adj)
high-priced (adj)	part-time (adj) **	twelve-year-old (adj)
internationally recognized (adj)	slow-moving (adj)	

Academic words

approximately (adv) **	implement (v) **	strategy (n) ***
commitment (n) ***	monitor (v) **	visual (adj) **

Academic words review

Complete the sentences using words from the box.

commitment	implement	restored	source	visual

1 It will be extremely difficult to _____ the change without the full support of the board.
2 The painting has been recently _____ and is now on show to the public.
3 Getting married is a big _____ and changes your life.
4 The _____ effects in the latest George Carpenter film are incredible.
5 The _____ of the White Nile was discovered by the German explorer, Burkhart Waldecker.

Unit review

Listening 1		I can listen for specific information.
Listening 2		I can understand priorities.
Study skill		I can use abbreviations in note-making.
Vocabulary		I can use compound adjectives.
Grammar		I can use complex passive sentences.
Speaking		I can voice and allay concerns.

Discussion point

Discuss with a partner.

1 How long do you spend looking at your cell phone every day? Are you worried this will affect your health?

2 What other kind of health problems are increasing as a result of modern technology?

3 What do you do to stay healthy?

Medical issues for the 21st century

Hearing loss

It's estimated that 15% of teenagers in the U.K. suffer from hearing loss caused by personal headphone use.

Obesity

People who work over 40 hours a week are about 8% more likely to be obese.

Back and neck pain

Smartphone users spend an average of 3.5 hours a day looking at their phone—something that can lead to neck and back pain.

Anxiety

57% of people surveyed feel anxious when unable to access their mobile phone.

Stomach pains

In a 2011 study, 16% of smartphones were contaminated with E-coli, a bacterium that causes stomach pains and food poisoning.[1]

VIDEO

A BUZZ IN MEDICINE

Before you watch

Match the words in bold with the correct definitions.

1	**antibiotics** (n)	a	not harmed or affected by something
2	**bacteria** (n)	b	medicine which helps cure infections
3	**die out** (phr. v)	c	to give someone medical care
4	**resistant** (adj)	d	tiny living organisms which cause diseases or decay
5	**treat** (v)	e	very serious injury to your skin
6	**wound** (n)	f	to become less common, then disappear completely

UNIT AIMS

LISTENING 1 Listening to categorize information
LISTENING 2 Listening to understand cause-and-effect relationships
STUDY SKILL Chairing a group

VOCABULARY Medical language
GRAMMAR Past modals of deduction
SPEAKING Asking to clarify or confirm ideas you hear

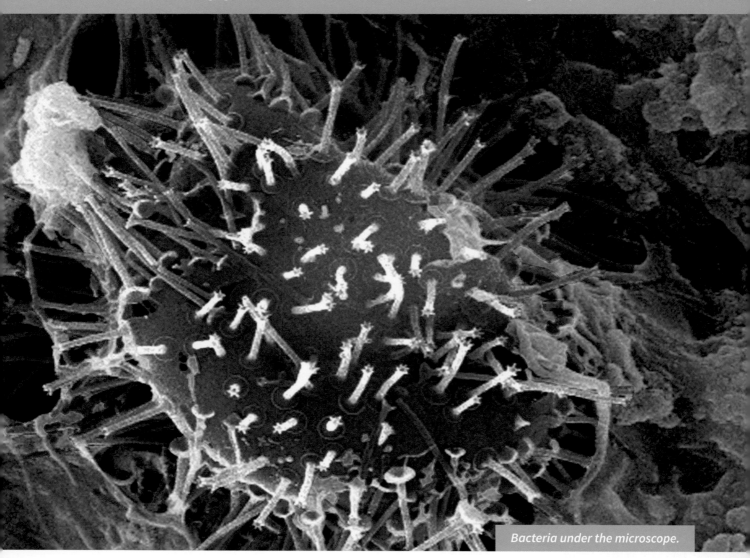

Bacteria under the microscope.

While you watch

Watch the video and choose *T* (True) or *F* (False).

1 Natural honey loses its "good bacteria" when processed.　　　　T / F

2 Bacteria and honey are combined to form the medicine.　　　　T / F

3 The medicine has been successfully tested on horses.　　　　T / F

4 The team have discovered 30 different bacteria.　　　　T / F

After you watch

Work with a partner. Discuss the questions.

1 Can you think of other medicines that have come from animals and plants?

2 Do you think it is important to study medicines made from plants and animals?

   Yes, it is very important because …

   No, I don't think it is so important because …

3 Why is the discovery of using honey important for medicine?

   I think it is important because …

   There are many reasons why …

Germ myths

A Vocabulary preview

1 Read the sentences. Match the words in bold with the correct definitions.

1 It's a **myth** that being cold can give you a cold. Don't believe it.
2 There might be a high **concentration** of germs on that wet sponge.
3 Air **circulates** in an airplane during a flight.
4 It's a **germ** that causes sore throats.
5 After a meal, it takes at least several hours to **digest** all the food.
6 Some bacteria are **harmful**, but "good" bacteria help us.
7 Water from the faucet in this area is **unsafe** to drink.
8 The flu can be **transmitted** by someone coughing and sneezing.

a (n) a large amount of something in one place
b (n) a story many people believe, but which is not true
c (n) a small living thing that causes diseases
d (v) to move around continuously (within a system)
e (adj) causing hurt or damage
f (v) to change food to a form the body can use
g (adj) dangerous
h (v) to send or pass something from one person or place to another

2 Complete the sentences using the words in bold from Exercise 1.

1 It's _____ to eat meat that hasn't been properly cooked.
2 It's widely recognized that smoking is _____ to the body.
3 The virus was _____ by people coughing near one another.
4 It's important to wash your hands to stop the spread of _____.
5 Please open the window so that the air _____ a bit.
6 Phones often contain a high _____ of bacteria.
7 Some bacteria help us to _____ food.
8 It might just be a _____, but many people believe it.

GLOSSARY

tuberculosis (n) a serious infectious disease that affects the lungs

virus (n) an infectious living thing that causes disease or illness

B Before you listen

1 Work with a partner. Decide if the following statements are facts (based on evidence) or myths (ideas that are not true, but believed by many). Write *F* (fact) or *M* (myth).

1 —— Vitamin C prevents colds.

2 —— To stay healthy, we need to get plenty of sleep.

3 —— An influenza shot can give you influenza.

4 —— We need to drink eight glasses of water a day to be healthy.

5 —— Sitting too close to the computer ruins your eyes.

6 —— A healthy breakfast is important.

2 Work with a partner. Discuss other medical myths or facts you know.

C Global listening

When discussing categories of information, a speaker will often repeat certain key words to help you understand the categories. Pay attention to these key words. After you finish listening, you can review the ideas in each category to help you to understand the main ideas of what you heard.

🎧 6.1 Listen to *Germ myths* and answer the questions.

1 The main focus of the podcast is that …

a there are germs everywhere.

b there are ideas about germs that aren't correct.

c there are germs in many public places.

2 Why does the speaker mention "good bacteria"?

a To illustrate bacteria are everywhere.

b To show some bacteria aren't harmful.

c To indicate bacteria are on all food.

3 According to the podcast, what is one myth about airplanes?

a People get sick from other passengers.

b People get sick because the air is cool.

c People get sick because the air recirculates.

4 The speaker believes that the "Five-second rule" is …

a reasonable.   b a myth.   c true.

5 Which of the following is not discussed on the podcast?

a germs on money   b germs on airplanes   c germs on keyboards

Listening for detail

D Close listening

🎧 **6.1** Listen to *Germ myths* again and complete the notes with no more than two words or a number.

GERM MYTHS

GENERAL INFO

[1]_____ = bacteria and viruses that can cause disease.

Most germs are [2]_____ to us!

MONEY

[3]_____ and [4]_____ pick up bacteria / viruses as they circulate.

Level of bacteria depends on age + what it's [5]_____.

Don't worry about this – just wash your hands!

RECIRCULATED AIR

Air filters on planes remove roughly [6]_____% of bacteria and viruses.

Plane air refreshed [7]_____ times an hour > office air refreshed [8]_____ times an hour.

Don't worry about this either – recirculated air = unlikely to make you sick.

KITCHENS

Kitchens = full of germs! Cleaning with sponges + cloths may [9]_____ germs.

Floor has a high concentration of germs.

"Five-second rule" = a myth. Any food dropped on the floor is [10]_____ to eat.

E Critical thinking

Work in a group. Discuss the questions.

1 Do you disagree with any of the claims made on the podcast? Why?

2 How would you alter your behavior on a flight based on the podcast?

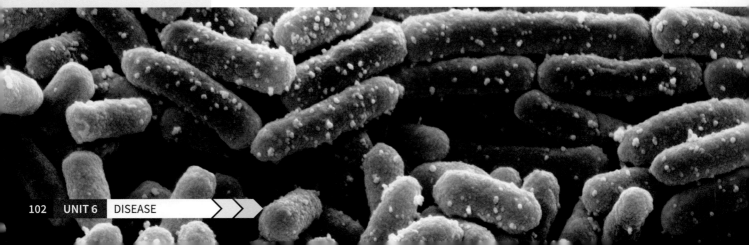

Study skills   Chairing a group

When working in a group, find out the range of skills and experience in the group. Who prefers to organize, run meetings, write? For each session, decide who will take which role.

Chairperson

Although everybody should help, the chair helps the group to draw up an agenda and keep to it, ensures that everyone gets to speak and that their views are heard, keeps the group focused on the point being discussed, and sums up the main points.

© Stella Cottrell (2013)

1   Work with a partner. Discuss the questions.

   1   What do you enjoy in group discussions?

   2   What factors make a group discussion difficult to participate in?

   3   What qualities are important in a group leader?

2   Work in a group. Discuss what Ahmed is doing right / wrong when leading a group discussion.

Ahmed has been chosen to lead the study session. He hasn't done it before and he is nervous about being able to do a good job. Before the session, he makes a list of questions to talk about. At the beginning, he talks for a long time about his own ideas. Then, he asks the other members for their ideas. His classmates all start talking at once. He is excited because it seems like they are having a lively discussion. Then, he notices one of his classmates hasn't said anything. He stops the discussion and asks that classmate a question. When a different classmate starts to answer, he tells him to let the first classmate answer without being interrupted. At the end, Ahmed wants to review the main ideas of their discussion, but realizes no one was taking notes.

3   Look through these suggestions for being an effective group leader. Work with a partner to discuss why they are important.

   1   Prepare for the discussion by organizing what the group will talk about.

   2   Ask questions to start the discussion and to keep it going, but don't dominate the discussion.

   3   Make sure everyone has the chance to speak without interruptions.

   4   Make sure the group stays on topic.

   5   Encourage everyone to ask questions and to confirm that they understood ideas correctly.

   6   Ask someone to take notes on the discussion.

   7   Review the notes to check they cover the main points discussed.

2 LISTENING

Disease detectives

A Vocabulary preview

1 Read the sentences. Match the words in bold with the correct definitions.

1 The Ebola virus **epidemic** in West Africa 2013–2016 killed over 11,000 people.

2 At the **peak** of the outbreak many people were sick.

3 At first, health care workers couldn't **figure out** why so many people were sick.

4 This podcast **concerns** some of the reasons why people gain weight.

5 Leading **researchers** in the field say that they're getting close to a cure for the disease.

6 The cause of the disease was **traced back to** drinking unsafe water.

7 There must have been a **toxin** in the plant. The animals that ate it became very sick.

8 The dodo was declared **extinct** in 1662.

a (v) to understand something after thinking about it

b (v) to be about a particular subject

c (n) the rapid spread of a disease among many people in one place

d (n) the time when something is at its highest

e (n) someone who studies a subject in detail and tries to discover new information about it

f (n) a poisonous substance

g (v) to find the origin of something

h (adj) no longer existing

2 Complete the sentences with words from Exercise 1. Change the form if necessary.

1 Pandas are an endangered species. Many are concerned they will become _____ unless they are protected.

2 _____ claim there is no causal relationship between taking Vitamin C and recovering from a cold.

3 They quickly _____ that the water was making the children sick.

4 The disease was _____ the 1700s.

5 Tests proved there were _____ in the rice.

6 The cholera _____ in 2010 was one of the worst in recent history.

7 At its _____, the disease affected over 800 people a day.

8 This article _____ diseases like malaria.

B Before you listen

Work with a partner. Look at the images below and answer the questions.

1 What kind of environments do these animals live in – land, water, or both?

2 What other animals live in similar environments?

3 How do you think these animals are connected to disease?

prawn   *snail*   *flying fox*

C Global listening

🎧 **6.2 Listen to *Disease detectives* and choose the best answer.**

1 What was the main challenge for the researchers?

  a Understanding the interests of the people.

  b Understanding why flying foxes were endangered.

  c Understanding the causes of the problems.

2 The main cause of the schistosomiasis outbreak in Senegal was …

  a the lack of medicine.

  b the construction of a new dam.

  c toxins in the meat.

3 Project Crevette was created to try to …

  a change the flow of the river.

  b give people medicine to treat the disease.

  c reintroduce prawns to the river.

4 The main cause of the lytico-bodig outbreak in Guam was …

  a toxins in the meat.

  b unclean water.

  c overhunting of the flying fox.

Listening for main ideas

GLOSSARY

dam (n) a wall built across a river to stop the water flowing

outbreak (n) the start or sudden appearance of disease or war

parasite (n) a plant or animal that lives in or on another animal to feed on it

Listening to understand
cause-and-effect
relationships

D Close listening

In lectures, speakers often need their audience to understand how actions cause results (or effects). Usually, these relationships are explicitly stated:

*The high concentration of the toxin **caused** the disease.*

***The result was** the disease disappeared completely.*

However, sometimes the relationships are only implied:

There were no cases of the disease before the dam was built. (The dam caused it.)

🎧 6.2 Listen to *Disease detectives* again. Choose *T* (True) or *F* (False). Then correct the false statements.

1	Schistosomiasis is caused by a parasite that lives in river prawns.	T / F
2	Construction of the Diama Dam changed the flow of the river.	T / F
3	The prawns' extinction was caused by changes to their habitat.	T / F
4	The snail population increased because they had no predators.	T / F
5	More snails in the river resulted in fewer cases of schistosomiasis.	T / F
6	Lytico-bodig was caused by a toxin in flour.	T / F
7	Disease led to a decline in the flying fox population.	T / F
8	Lytico-bodig disappeared when people stopped eating flying fox.	T / F

E Critical thinking

Work in a group. Discuss the questions.

1 What are the long-term environmental advantages of a solution like Project Crevette?

2 What are the various factors that should be considered in order to understand the outbreak of a disease?

3 What are good ways to prevent the spread of a disease? Compile a list of ways and then rank them.

Critical thinking

Either / or fallacies

In some statements, there are only two possible options:

You're either alive or dead. (This is true. You can only be one or the other. There are no other options.)

However, sometimes a speaker presents something as if there are only two choices, when many other choices are possible. This is named an **either / or fallacy**. For example:

You either agree with me or you don't. (This is not true. You might agree with some of my ideas, but not all of them.)

You either loved the movie or you hated it. (This is not true. You might have thought the movie was just "OK." You might have quite liked it, but not loved it.)

Being able to recognize **either / or fallacies** will help you to evaluate claims and information you hear.

1 🎧 6.3 Work with a partner. Listen to an extract from *Germ myths* and answer the questions.

   1 What is the either / or fallacy the host makes?
   2 Why is this not true?

2 Work with a partner. Discuss which are examples of true choices and which are either / or fallacies and why.

   1 Try not to worry about the interview. You'll either get the job or you won't.
   2 We either raise taxes or crime increases—it's your choice.
   3 In Spain, you're either a Barcelona fan or a Real Madrid fan.
   4 Look, you've either finished the assignment or you haven't.
   5 There are only two types of people in the world—those who like getting up early and those who don't.
   6 There's no excuse for unemployment. If you don't have a job, you must be lazy.

3 Work in a group. Discuss the questions.

   1 Why is it important to recognize either / or fallacies?
   2 Why do you think people often use either / or fallacies in discussions and debates?
   3 In what other situations are either / or fallacies used?

Vocabulary development

Medical language

1   Read the sentences. Match the words and phrases in bold with the correct definitions.

   1   His stomach began to **ache** and he shivered from the cold.

   2   Luckily, the **infection** hasn't spread to the lungs.

   3   The good news is that the condition isn't **life-threatening**.

   4   I'm going to the doctor's on Thursday for a **check-up**.

   5   My daughter's **come down with** influenza, so she won't be at school today.

   6   My father has a rare stomach **disorder** which can make it painful to eat.

   7   The doctor gave the patient some medicine to **treat** his fever and chills.

   8   The doctor said it was **critical** that the patient go to the hospital.

   a   (v) to become ill

   b   (n) an illness caused by bacteria or a virus that affects one part of the body

   c   (v) to have a continuous pain in one part of your body

   d   (adj) likely to cause death

   e   (n) a general medical examination to make sure you are healthy

   f   (v) to give medical care to someone for an illness or injury

   g   (n) an illness that causes a part of the body to stop working normally

   h   (adj) very important or very serious

2   Complete the sentences with words from Exercise 1. Change the form if necessary.

   1   When was the last time you went for a _____?

   2   Ebola is a rare disease that can be _____.

   3   "It's _____ that you take these tablets twice a day."

   4   The woman _____ influenza and had to stay home for a week.

   5   He developed an _____ because he didn't keep the cut clean.

   6   His legs _____, but he was glad to be home.

   7   The best way to _____ a cold is to sleep and drink tea.

   8   He has a rare blood _____ that makes it difficult to breathe.

3   Work with a partner. Discuss the questions.

   1   When was the last time you came down with an illness?

   2   How often do you go for a check-up?

   3   What's the best way to treat a cold?

Academic words

1 Match the words in bold with the correct definitions.

1	**assess** (v)	a	to change often
2	**clarify** (v)	b	the number of times something happens
3	**eliminate** (v)	c	based on strong reasons or facts
4	**incidence** (n)	d	to remove something that is not wanted or needed
5	**reinforce** (v)	e	to explain something more clearly to make it easier to understand
6	**valid** (adj)	f	to do something to make an opinion, statement, etc. stronger or to support it
7	**vary** (v)	g	to make a judgment about a person or situation after thinking carefully about it

2 Complete the sentences using the words in bold from Exercise 1.

1 I think having influenza is a _____ excuse for not coming to work.

2 It's important to _____ what you eat from day to day.

3 Researchers are working hard to _____ cancer.

4 There was an increased _____ of cholera after the natural disaster.

5 To _____, there is no cure for the common cold.

6 In a check-up, doctors _____ your general health.

7 These figures _____ the need for a better health program.

3 Work with a partner. Discuss the questions.

1 What do you think is a valid excuse for staying home?

2 Why is it important to vary your diet?

3 Are there any diseases you think we will never fully eliminate?

Speaking model

You are going to learn about using past modals of deduction, and about ways to clarify and confirm ideas you hear, including how to use the correct intonation on tag questions. You are then going to work in groups to use the modals of deduction to make a medical diagnosis and present your results.

A Analyze

Read the conversation and answer the questions below.

Luis: To get started, let's look at the situation. A man woke up one morning. He was very hot and the skin on his face was red. He also had a headache and felt very weak. Is this correct?

Elsa: Yes, he had a headache. He also had a slight fever and was very thirsty.

Filip: Those are classic influenza symptoms. It sounds like he might have caught influenza, doesn't it?

Luis: Or maybe he could have had a bad cold. That could cause a headache and fever, couldn't it? I feel thirsty, and need to drink more water and tea when I have a cold.

Elsa: That's true. But, we need to consider that the skin on his face was very red. His eyes were red too. Symptoms vary, of course, but it doesn't seem like influenza.

Luis: OK. Let's eliminate influenza as a possibility. He might have eaten something he was sensitive to. He had a reaction to some food, or to something he drank. That seems reasonable, doesn't it?

Filip: Sure, that's possible. But we also know that he works outdoors all day in the hot sun. He could have had a very bad sunburn, couldn't he?

Elsa: That doesn't seem right, does it? Do you mean a sunburn could cause his fever and headache? It couldn't have been just a bad sunburn.

Filip: Sure, it could have been. A bad sunburn can be serious. It can make people feel very sick.

Elsa: Umm. I still think it can't have been a sunburn. Let's consider how a doctor might assess the man's symptoms.

1 What were the man's symptoms?
2 What were the four explanations the group thought of?

B Discuss

Work with a partner. Discuss the questions.

1 Which of the explanations seems the best? Give reasons.
2 What else could have caused the man's symptoms?
3 Imagine the symptoms were caused by a bad sunburn. What could the man have done to prevent it?

Grammar

Past modals of deduction

We use modals of deduction to make predictions or guesses about what happened in the past.

Use *may / might / could* + *have* + past participle to say you think something is possible, but aren't sure:

The disease may / might / could have been spread by the water.

Use *must / had to* + *have* + past participle to say you are sure something is true because there is strong evidence:

The snails must have spread the disease.

The water had to have spread the disease.

Use *can't / couldn't* + *have* + past participle to say you're sure something isn't true:

That can't have been the cause.

The disease couldn't have started there.

1   Choose the correct modal verb to complete the sentences.

1   It's not clear what led to the decline. It **must** / **might** have died out naturally.

2   It **must** / **can't** have been food poisoning, because not everyone got sick.

3   The water **must** / **could** have been contaminated. There aren't any other possibilities.

4   We're not sure. Several factors **may** / **must** have led to the outbreak.

5   Alicia **could** / **couldn't** have been sick yesterday because I saw her at the gym.

2   Work with a partner. Read the sentences and make deductions using past modals.

1   Erin became ill after a business trip abroad.

2   Hundreds of people got sick after eating at the same restaurant.

3   Molly collapsed after finishing the marathon.

Speaking skill

To **clarify** an idea means to ask a question to find out if you understood the idea clearly. To **confirm** an idea means that you say what you understood, and then you ask if you understood the idea correctly. These are both very useful strategies in discussions.

To clarify an idea

Do you mean …? What do you mean by …? Could you clarify … for me?

To confirm an idea

So, you mean that …? I understood that … Is this correct?

So, your (main) point is …? You just explained why …, correct?

1   🔊 6.4 Listen to the conversation. Match the two halves to form questions.

1	What exactly do you mean	a	that disease is caused by stress?
2	So, your point is	b	how his health improved?
3	So, you mean	c	by environmental factors?
4	Could you clarify for me	d	you think stress was the biggest factor?

2   What is the speaker's conclusion about the relationship between stress and disease? Do you agree?

3   Work in a group. Discuss the following statements. Give reasons to support your ideas. Clarify and confirm ideas you hear.

1   A healthy diet and regular exercise help to prevent disease.

   A: A healthy diet means …

   B: So, you mean, you think people should eat …?

2   It is important to find good ways to relax and reduce stress.

   A: One way to relax is …

   B: So, you're saying it's a good idea to …

Pronunciation for speaking

Intonation with tag questions

When we use tag questions such as *didn't they?* and *is it?* we use either rising or falling intonation, depending on the meaning we want to express.

We use rising intonation to ask a genuine question:

That hurts, doesn't it? (I'm not sure, but it looks painful.)

We use falling intonation when we are already fairly sure of the answer:

That hurts, doesn't it? (I know it hurts because I've done the same thing!)

1 🎧 6.5 Listen and complete the tag questions.

1

A: The fever could have been from a cold, _____?

B: Sure, but colds don't usually cause fevers, _____?

A: Not always, but sometimes.

2

A: The patient got worse, _____?

B: No, she got better once the doctors treated her with some strong medicine.

3

A: It was difficult to diagnose the problem, _____?

B: Right. The doctors had a difficult time.

4

A: The symptoms started a few days later, _____?

B: No. It was about a week later or so.

2 🎧 6.5 Listen again and mark whether each question is said with a rising or falling intonation. Then practice the conversations with a partner.

Speaking task

Make deductions about how a disease in a medical case study might have been spread and what could have been done to prevent it. Then present your findings to the class.

Read

Imagine you are part of a medical team. Read the case study.

A woman in London went to an airport to pick up a friend returning from a trip to India. Her friend's flight was late, so she decided to eat dinner and have a cup of tea while she waited. About a week later, the woman started to get sick. At first, she just had a headache, but then she developed a fever. She had chills and was also very tired. She went to the doctor and was told she had influenza.

She took medication, but continued to get worse. Finally, after visiting several other doctors, she was diagnosed as having malaria. The woman couldn't understand how she could possibly have been exposed to malaria, which is transmitted by mosquitoes. Over 100 countries worldwide have a risk for malaria, but not England. In addition, she hadn't traveled anywhere for a year.

Plan

Think about possible explanations for how the woman might have become ill and what she could have done differently to avoiding becoming ill. Take notes. Organize your ideas in the chart.

Speak

Work in a group. Take turns presenting your ideas. Clarify and confirm the ideas you hear. Use tag questions to make sure you understand everything correctly. Decide together on the best explanation for why the woman came down with malaria.

Share

Have someone in your group present your group's explanation to the whole class. Compare ideas. Clarify other groups' explanations. Vote on the best explanation.

Reflect

Work with a partner. Discuss the questions.

1 How can we stop people believing medical myths such as Vitamin C prevents colds?
2 What can you do to help stop the spread of disease in your country?

Review

Wordlist

MACMILLAN
DICTIONARY

Vocabulary preview

circulate (v) **	epidemic (n)	harmful (adj) *	toxin (n)
concentration (n) ***	extinct (adj) *	myth (n) **	trace back to (phr v)
concern (v) ***	figure out (phr v)	peak (n) **	transmit (v) **
digest (v) *	germ (n)	researcher (n)	unsafe (adj)

Vocabulary development

ache (v) *	come down with (phr v)	disorder (n) **	life-threatening (adj)
check-up (n)	critical (adj) ***	infection (n) **	treat (v) ***

Academic words

assess (v) **	eliminate (v) **	reinforce (v) **	vary (v) ***
clarify (v) *	incidence (n) *	valid (adj) **	

Academic words review

Complete the sentences using words from the box.

assessed	eliminated	intelligence	reinforce	vary

1 After the earthquake, structural engineers _____ the damage to the town's buildings, and bridges.
2 Whilst the details may _____, the basic concept remains the same.
3 The iPhone personal assistant Siri, is one example of artificial _____.
4 These findings seem to _____ the idea that stress affects short-term memory.
5 Many infectious diseases have been almost entirely _____.

Unit review

Listening 1		I can categorize information.
Listening 2		I can understand cause-and-effect relationships.
Study skill		I can chair a group discussion.
Vocabulary		I can use medical language.
Grammar		I can use past modals of deduction.
Speaking		I can ask questions to clarify or confirm the ideas I hear.

7 SURVIVAL

Discussion point

Discuss with a partner.

1 What does the phrase "Think green" mean to you?

2 Which of the suggestions in the infographic do you already do? Which don't you do?

3 How are the 3Rs related to survival?

THINK GREEN—THE 3 Rs

REDUCE

Unplug your chargers.
Use energy-efficient lightbulbs.
Conserve water—take shorter showers.

REUSE

Repair things instead of replacing them.
Donate old clothes, books, and appliances to charity.
Use refillable water bottles.

RECYCLE

Recycle paper, cardboard, plastic, glass, and metal.
Avoid packaging that can't be recycled.

VIDEO

RAISING AWARENESS

Before you watch

Match the words in bold with the correct definitions.

1 **extinct** (adj)

2 **ivory** (n)

3 **orphans** (n)

4 **poaching** (n)

5 **tusks** (n)

a white material that elephants' long, pointed teeth are made from

b no longer existing

c babies without parents

d the illegal killing of animals (e.g. for meat, fur, or ivory)

e long, pointed teeth on animals such as elephants

UNIT AIMS

LISTENING 1 Predicting content using prior knowledge
LISTENING 2 Listening for language that connects ideas
STUDY SKILL Being effective in group discussions: playing your part

VOCABULARY Using word families
GRAMMAR The present unreal conditional
SPEAKING Contributing additional information to a discussion

A Chinese recycling plant.

While you watch

Watch the video and choose *T* (True) or *F* (False).

1 Baby elephants are poached for their ivory tusks. T / F

2 The elephant keeper says the number of orphan elephants is decreasing. T / F

3 Poaching could lead to elephants' extinction in Africa. T / F

4 Currently, every 10 minutes an elephant dies in Africa. T / F

5 In 10 or 15 years the wild elephants will be gone. T / F

After you watch

Work with a partner. Discuss the questions.

1 Do you think it's important to save elephants? Why? / Why not?

2 The CEO of Wildlife Direct says that when adult elephants are killed, you are removing the knowledge base of generations. What do you think this means for future generations of elephants?

Kindness as a survival skill

A Vocabulary preview

1 Match the words in bold with the correct definitions.

1 They realized that without food or water, their chances of **survival** were low.
2 Government aid will **ensure** the local area recovers quickly from the flood.
3 The organization relies on the **generosity** of strangers.
4 Local residents **gathered** in the town square to offer their support.
5 Thousands of employees were **laid off** after the disaster.
6 **Kindness** to one another is important in many situations.
7 The **desire** for survival is very strong for most people.
8 By helping each other, the neighbors formed a **bond** that lasted for years.

a (n) willingness to give time, money, help, etc.
b (n) helpful, caring behavior
c (n) a strong hope or wish
d (n) a feeling or interest that joins people together
e (phr v) to stop employing someone, often because there isn't enough work for them
f (n) the state of continuing to live
g (v) to make certain that something happens or is done
h (v) to come together in one place to see or do something

2 Complete the sentences with the words in bold from Exercise 1.

1 Crowds of people _____ in front of the aid workers' tents.
2 His _____ made it possible to rebuild the surgery.
3 The government did many things to _____ the safety of the people in cities.
4 After five days, the _____ of the earthquake victims looked doubtful.
5 My father was _____ after they closed the factory.
6 She showed us great _____ during a difficult time.
7 His _____ for water pushed him to keep walking.
8 During an emergency, a _____ is often formed between victims.

B Before you listen

Use your own experiences and knowledge about a topic to predict what you are going to hear.

This will help you prepare for the listening and will get you thinking about the topics and issues that are likely to be covered. Use the title, any visuals, and read the questions to help you prepare.

Predict content using prior knowledge

Work with a partner. Discuss the questions.

1   Read the title of this listening section. How might kindness be a survival skill?

2   What kind acts do you think you might hear about? Share your ideas with a partner.

C Global listening

🔊 **7.1** Listen to *Kindness as a survival skill* and circle the phrases that best complete the sentences.

1   The woman decided to leave extra money at the café because she was **very wealthy / concerned about her neighbors**.

2   A man helps fix the roof of his neighbor's house. The following week the neighbor helps him in his back yard. This is an example of **direct / indirect** reciprocity.

3   The café story is about **direct / indirect** reciprocity because the people who gave money **expected / didn't expect** a particular person to help them out.

4   The speaker believes people help after a natural disaster because we **expect direct reciprocity in the future / naturally help one another to survive**.

5   The man who saved children from the river risked his life because he **wanted to be a hero / knew it was the right thing to do**.

Listening for main ideas

GLOSSARY

reciprocity (n) the act of exchanging things with others because it helps you both

D Close listening

1 🎧 7.1 Listen to *Kindness as a survival skill* again. Circle the correct answer.

1 The speaker defines "direct reciprocity" as:

a a bond.

b trust.

c a specific exchange.

2 According to the speaker, indirect reciprocity works because:

a people ask for money.

b people feel they can ask for help.

c people distribute supplies.

3 Food, water, and medical supplies are mentioned as examples of:

a direct reciprocity.

b emergency aid.

c risks people take.

2 🎧 7.1 Listen to *Kindness as a survival skill* again and choose *T* (True) or *F* (False).

1 The woman at the café was the only customer to leave money.   T / F

2 The speaker refers to bonds within families as well as
between friends.   T / F

3 The natural disasters mentioned are earthquakes, floods, and
forest fires.   T / F

4 The car in the river had three children in it.   T / F

5 The speaker concludes that building communities is essential
for survival.   T / F

E Critical thinking

Work in a group. Discuss the questions.

1 What reasons does the speaker in the podcast give for why reciprocity is important? Which reason do you think is the most important?

2 Can you think of examples of direct and indirect reciprocity from your own lives, or those of people you know of?

Study skills | Being effective in group discussions: playing your part

Discussion sessions in class, or within groups are most effective when everyone makes a contribution. This requires each student to take personal responsibility for creating the kind of environment where everyone has a chance to contribute, having the courage, and making an effort to contribute.

Are you someone who needs to focus more on:

- creating the space for yourself to speak, and making more of a contribution in class / groups?
- leaving more space for others to speak?

© Stella Cottrell (2013)

1   Work with a partner. Discuss the questions.

1   When are discussion sessions most effective?

2   What does "make a contribution" mean here?

3   What are the two ways a student can take personal responsibility in the discussion?

2   Match the problems (1–5) with the advice (a–e).

1   I always feel like I'm doing all of the talking.

2   I can never remember what I want to say.

3   No one seems to follow the ideas I share.

4   I get so nervous every time I try to speak.

5   Sometimes the ideas I hear seem irrelevant, so I stop listening, and have trouble joining back in.

a   Make a list of the points you want to make and any supporting evidence.

b   Try to relax, and act confidently even if you don't feel that way.

c   By paying attention to what other students say, it can help you clarify your own position.

d   Ask other people questions to encourage them to join in the discussion.

e   Try to speak up, and talk clearly so everyone can hear what you are saying.

3   Work with a partner. Discuss the questions.

1   What are your strengths in group discussions?

2   What are your biggest challenges in groups?

3   What do you think you might do to be more effective?

Building for the future

A Vocabulary preview

1 Choose the correct definition for the words in bold.

1 The government provided money to **construct** more housing in the city.

    a to build   b to consider

2 The house was **converted into** a doctor's office.

    a to change from one purpose to another   b to provide supplies for

3 The company **emphasizes** that it uses local building materials.

    a to say in a polite way   b to show something is important

4 A rough **estimate** of the population of Istanbul is about 15 million people.

    a a good guess, not exact   b a possible explanation

5 The building was **designed to** use solar energy to heat it.

    a shown to have   b planned for a purpose

6 The country had a strong economy because it had many natural **resources.**

    a land, trees, water to use   b places to go

7 The construction company had planned to only use recycled stone for the porch, but then decided to build the **entire** house with recycled materials.

    a modern   b whole

8 We need to consider people's **current** needs not just future needs.

    a important   b present

2 Complete the sentences with the words in bold from Exercise 1.

1 The old school was _____ a community center.

2 The cost _____ was too low. The builder hadn't considered transportation costs.

3 The library was _____ use a lot of natural light.

4 Oil and water are considered important natural _____.

5 The company wanted to use local materials to _____ the houses.

6 The _____ need for housing in the city is a serious problem.

7 The _____ building was built from recycled materials.

8 Green building _____ being environmentally responsible.

B Before you listen

Activating prior knowledge

One challenge for the 21st century is to design housing to meet growing needs. Discuss with a partner how the following areas influence today's architects when they design new housing.

cost   demand   energy use   limited global resources

C Global listening

1 **7.2 Complete the summary with the words in the box. Then listen to** *Building for the future* **and check.**

environmentally responsible   in the future
it is used   new purposes   resources wisely

The building challenge we face is to meet the needs of people both now, and
¹_____. Because there are limited resources, we need to design
buildings that use ²_____. The main goals of green building are
based on being ³_____ both when a building is constructed as well
as when ⁴_____. Reusing existing buildings for ⁵_____ is
also a good way to save limited natural resources like wood, and metal.

A lecture or presentation may have several subtopics, which contribute
information to help you to understand the main topic. At the beginning
of the presentation, the speaker often presents the main topic, and the
subtopics, so that you will know how the presentation is organized. For
example:

Today we're talking about green building. (main topic)

We're going to focus on energy use (subtopic) *and building reuse …*
(subtopic)

To make a transition from one subtopic to the next, the speaker will often
use phases such as: *Regarding …, / As for …, / Turning to …, / Another
important consideration is ….*

Paying attention to these phrases will help you know when the speaker is
moving from one subtopic to the next.

Listening for phrases
that connect ideas

2 **Listen again. Match the connecting phrases with the subtopics they connect.**

1 With this in mind …
2 Regarding the …
3 Now let's look at …
4 Taking that into consideration …

a current challenge ➜ the trend of "green" building   ___
b overview of presentation ➜ the principles of green building   ___
c principles of green building ➜ energy use   ___
d new "green" construction ➜ building reuse   ___

D Close listening

🎧 7.2 Listen to *Building for the future* again, and complete the table using no more than three words in each blank.

Principles of green building	Five principles 1 = building is [1]_____ 2 = [2]_____ well with surroundings 3 = not waste resources 4 = meets the [3]_____ of the people 5 = better to [4]_____ an old building than [5]_____ a new one
Design considerations	It must be [6]_____ for the people who use it. Germany: windows + landscaping designed to take advantage of winter sun > more [7]_____ windows for light, and warmth. Egypt: buildings designed to allow less [8]_____ in at midday, but enough natural light for people to see > trees planted to [9]_____ sunlight + reduce the [10]_____ required to keep buildings cool.

E Critical thinking

Work in a group. Discuss the questions.

1 Which renewable sources of energy do you think would work well in your country? Why?

2 What types of building materials are not renewable? What could they be replaced with?

Critical thinking

Strengthening an argument

An argument is an opinion or claim supported by evidence. Any evidence you include should clearly strengthen your argument. Avoid evidence that is related to the general topic, but doesn't directly strengthen your argument, as well as information that could potentially weaken your position.

1   Read an extract from *Building for the future*. Answer the questions.

> Our ability to survive in the future depends in part on how we adapt the way we currently construct buildings. Estimates are that by the year 2050, there will be 9 billion people in the world. If we had unlimited resources of building materials, water, and energy, this wouldn't be a concern. But we don't. Thus, the challenge now is to learn to design buildings that use resources well.

1   What is the argument being made?
2   What is the supporting evidence?

2   Work with a partner. Which of the statements below strengthens the argument in Exercise 1? Why?

1   A wide variety of global building materials is currently available.
2   Sand, an essential ingredient in concrete, is being extracted faster than it's being replaced.
3   Many new apartment buildings have been constructed in China in recent years.

3   Work with a partner. Read the arguments and potential evidence. Write *S* if the evidence strengthens the argument, *W* if it weakens it, and *I* if it's irrelevant.

1   Renewable energy is energy that comes from natural sources, such as sunlight and wind. It is a free source of energy that has many advantages.
    a   ___ Solar energy can be used to heat and cool as well as for lighting, and generating electricity.
    b   ___ In many parts of the world, coal and gas are used to produce electricity.
    c   ___ The cost of using solar panels for homes is still too high for many people to afford.

2   In car accidents, certain factors affect your chances of survival. For example, research shows survival is less likely if the collision is head-on.
    a   ___ Countries vary on seat belt laws. Some require drivers to use them, while some don't.
    b   ___ The data shows that wearing a seat belt and having air bags in the car definitely save lives.
    c   ___ Due to factors such as the type of road and the time of day, researchers are unable to conclude why some people survive, and others don't.

Vocabulary development

Learning word families

When you learn a new word, you can increase your vocabulary further by learning the other parts of speech related to the word.

Verb	Noun(s)	Adjective	Adverb
specify	specification	specific	specifically
consider	consideration	considerate	considerately
create	creation / creativity	creative	creatively
cooperate	cooperation	cooperative	cooperatively
recycle	recycling	recycled	–
–	medicine / medication	medical	medically
survive	survivor / survival	–	–
1_____	risk	2_____	3_____
–	generosity	4_____	5_____
encourage	6_____	7_____	8_____

1 **Complete the sentences with the correct form of the words in parentheses. Use the table above to help you.**

1 The design of the house was changed to meet the _____ (specify) needs of the people living there.

2 The families worked _____ (cooperate) to help their community after the flood.

3 After the accident, there was only one _____ (survive). The doctors were amazed he was able to live for two days before help came.

4 The people in the community needed to be _____ (consider), and not use too much water.

5 Using recycled building materials is a _____ (create) way to save limited resources.

6 _____ (recycle) companies are increasing worldwide as people become aware of the need to be environmentally responsible.

2 **Complete the word families in the skills box.**

Academic words

1 Choose the correct definition for the words in bold.

1 There had been no rain. The town had to **adapt** to having less water to use.

   a to not allow yourself to do something   b to change to fit a new situation

2 The emergency team rushed to **respond** to the earthquake victims.

   a to react to something said or done   b to persuade someone

3 After a natural disaster, people often **contribute** to an emergency fund.

   a to have power over   b to give to something to help others

4 The project will go faster if everyone decides to **cooperate.**

   a to have something as the main feature   b to work together for the same goal

5 The global **economy** is growing every year.

   a the money a country makes from industry and trade   b the way prices increase

6 The government decided to **expand** the emergency plan to include more doctors.

   a to reduce the impact of   b to make greater in size or importance

7 The designers used new colors and soft lighting to **transform** the room into a relaxing space.

   a to change completely   b to move from one place to another

2 Complete the sentences with the words in bold from Exercise 1.

1 The builders decided to _____ the house to make it bigger than the original plan.

2 The _____ in Asia can be affected by business decisions in Europe.

3 Experiencing a natural disaster can _____ a person's life forever.

4 If someone is born in a warm climate, it might be hard to _____ to a cold climate.

5 The people in the group didn't want to _____. They each did what they wanted to do.

6 One way to _____ is to give assistance. You don't need to give money.

3 Work in a group. Discuss the questions.

1 What are ways to contribute to help others?

2 How do people need to adapt when they become students?

3 If you had the opportunity to transform a public space, such as a park, or a building, what would you do?

Speaking model

You are going to learn about the present unreal conditional, ways of contributing additional information to a discussion, and question intonation. You are then going to use these to discuss the global water challenge.

A Analyze

Work with a partner. Read the model and answer the questions.

Jude:	The question "How can we use water more efficiently in daily life?" is an interesting one to discuss. Water is used in so many ways: in restaurants, in gardening, in manufacturing, in agriculture, right? As I understand it, some water can be re-used from buildings. I don't know much about manufacturing or agriculture, though. We should do some research, and then come up with suggestions on ways to save water.
Bea:	That's a good idea. For now, let's focus instead on specific ways to reduce water use at home. I think that we all waste a lot more water than we realize. For example, if we turned the faucet off when brushing our teeth, or washing our hands, we'd use a lot less water.
Al:	Does your family have a dishwasher? I recently read that a dishwasher uses less water, and less energy than doing dishes by hand. That surprised me.
Jude:	Sadly, we don't have a dishwasher, so I'll have to think of other ways to save water.
Al:	Well you could save a lot of water if you took shorter showers … sometimes you're in there for half an hour!
Jude:	Haha! That's definitely something I could do. What else?
Bea:	Well, my family collects rain water…
Al:	Really? What for?
Bea:	To water the plants in the yard. It saves having to use water from the faucet every time.
Jude:	That's a great idea.
Bea:	Yeah, it's pretty easy to do. You should try it.
Jude:	I would, but I don't have a yard!

1　Which four areas of water use does Jude mention?
2　Who gives a hypothetical example of how to save bathroom water?
3　Who gives a real-world example for how to solve a problem?

B Discuss

Work with a partner. Discuss the questions.

1　Which of the water-saving ideas in the model surprised you? Which would you consider trying?
2　What are other ways to reduce water use at home where you live?

Grammar

> ### The present unreal conditional
>
> We use the present unreal conditional to talk about imagined or impossible situations:
>
> If + past simple / would + base form
>
> *If I won a lot of money, I'd donate some to charity.*
>
> *You'd save electricity if you unplugged your TV at night.*
>
> With the verb *be*, we use *were* for all subjects:
>
> *If electric cars were cheaper, more people would buy them.*
>
> We can also replace *would* with *might* / *could*:
>
> *You could save a lot of money if you used less water.*
>
> *If you recycled more, you might feel less guilty!*

1   Use the correct form of the verbs in parentheses to complete the conditional sentences.

   1   If people _____ (take) shorter showers, they _____ (waste) less water.

   2   If she _____ (have) more time, she _____ (take) care of her neighbor.

   3   If he _____ (close) the windows, it _____ (be) cooler in the house.

   4   If they _____ (turn off) the lights during the day, they _____ (save) energy.

   5   If they _____ (have) lots of water, they _____ (have to) worry about shortages.

2   Write conditional sentences using the information in parentheses.

   1   The village is very poor. (have money / build a well)

   2   The neighbors don't help one another. (help one another / have a stronger community)

   3   The builders don't use local materials. (use local materials / save resources)

   4   The houses aren't strong enough to withstand the earthquake. (be strong enough / people feel safer)

   5   The windows are very small. (be bigger / let in more light)

Speaking skill

Contributing additional information to a discussion

There are different ways you can contribute ideas to a discussion:

Your own knowledge

As far as I know,   *As I understand it,*   *What I've been told is …*

Your own idea and opinions

I think that …   *What I've found …*   *In my view …*

Other information you have heard or read

I recently read / heard that …   *There was a recent story about …*
I saw something on the Internet that said …

1 **7.3** Listen and check (✓) how each student contributes ideas to the discussion. Then summarize the main ideas with a partner.

Student	Own knowledge	Own opinion	Other information
1			
2			
3			
4			

2 Work in groups. Choose a recent event: local, national, or global. Discuss what you know about it. Encourage each other to contribute additional information to the discussion.

A: *I saw online that ….*

B: *As I understand it ….*

C: *In my view ….*

A: *Well, as far as I know…*

Pronunciation for speaking

> ## Question intonation
>
> Use falling intonation
>
> for *wh-* questions:
> *What is water used for where you live?*
>
> to indicate a choice between two things:
> *Is more water used for manufacturing or for farming?*
>
> Use rising intonation
>
> for *Yes / No* questions:
> *Are you concerned about global water use?*
>
> to change a statement to a question without changing the word order. This is often used to show surprise:
> *You don't think water shortage is a serious problem?*

1 🎧 7.4 Listen to the intonation in the following questions. Then listen again and repeat.

    1   Where does the city get its water from?

    2   Does the city process salt water to use for drinking water?

    3   That water is used for drinking?

    4   The village doesn't have any water?

    5   When do they usually have water shortages?

2 🎧 7.5 Listen to the conversations. Draw rising (↗) or falling (↘) arrows to mark the question intonation. Then practice the conversations with a partner.

    1 A: What are ways people can use less water at home?

        B: They can take shorter showers. They can re-use water.

    2 A: I read some cities get water from melting ice caps in the mountains.

        B: Cities get water from melting ice caps? I didn't know that.

    3 A: Are there really water shortages everywhere?

        B: Well, not absolutely everywhere, but it is a serious global problem.

    4 A: How can water be used efficiently in public buildings?

        B: One way is to collect rain water to use for landscaping.

Speaking task

Discuss the global water challenge and present your ideas to the class.

Brainstorm

Read the information. Then answer the questions in groups.

Experts have said that water is one of the biggest survival challenges of the 21st century. 70% of the Earth is covered by water, but 97% of that water is salt water. Of the other 3%, only 1% is available for people to use. Globally, four times as much water is used now as 50 years ago. This is primarily due to increases in world population, along with increases in manufacturing in developing countries, and to more large-scale agricultural practices. By 2050, it is predicted that about a quarter of the world's population will have regular water shortages. This is a global problem.

1 What is the predicted situation for 2050? What are the main causes?
2 Is the lack of water an issue where you live?
3 What are specific ways people can reduce water use at home?
4 What are some ways communities can re-use water, and use water efficiently in parks, gardens, and public buildings?
5 What are other ways of possibly getting access to fresh water besides desalinization (removing salt from seawater), or taking advantage of melting ice caps?

Plan

Work alone. Use a mind map to organize your ideas on what you consider the best ways to use water efficiently, and to meet the global water challenge.

Speak

Review your ideas in your group. Compare ideas and opinions, and contribute additional ideas to the discussion. Use unreal conditional sentences to discuss possible situations.

Share

Present your group's ideas to other classmates. Together, compile a list of ways people at home and in public can use water efficiently to meet the global challenge.

Reflect

Work with a partner. Discuss the questions.

1 How can social media be used effectively to help victims of natural disasters?
2 In addition to kindness, what other survival skills are important?

Review

Wordlist

MACMILLAN
DICTIONARY

Vocabulary preview

bond (n) **	be designed to (phr)	entire (adj) ***	kindness (n)
construct (v) ***	desire (n) ***	estimate (n) ***	lay off (phr v)
convert into (phr v)	emphasize (v) **	gather (v) ***	resource (n) ***
current (adj) ***	ensure (v) **	generosity (n)	survival (n) **

Vocabulary development

considerate (adj)	recycled (adj) *	specification (n) **
cooperatively (adv)	recycling (n) *	survivor (n) *

Academic words

adapt (v) **	cooperate (v) *	expand (v) ***	transform (v) **
contribute (v) ***	economy (n) ***	respond (v) ***	

Academic words review

Complete the sentences using words from the box.

adapted	approximately	clarify	expanded	monitor

1 When Rashid moved from a village to a large city, he quickly _____ to a different way of life.

2 Muscat is a city of _____ 1.5 million people.

3 I didn't understand our tutor's explanation, so I asked her to _____ it for me.

4 The study has been _____ to include residents aged over 60.

5 UN peacekeepers were sent to the country to _____ the elections and make sure they were fair.

Unit review

Listening 1	☐	I can predict content using prior knowledge.
Listening 2	☐	I can listen for language that connects ideas.
Study skill	☐	I can be effective in group discussions.
Vocabulary	☐	I can use word families.
Grammar	☐	I can use the unreal conditional.
Speaking	☐	I can contribute information to a discussion.

Cybercrime

Common types of cybercrime

Romance scammers:
Criminals target people on online dating sites, win their "love," and then ask for money. Annual cost to victims: $65 million

Auto scammers:
Thieves convince victims to pay for cars that don't exist. Annual cost to victims: $51 million

Real-estate scams:
Thieves try to persuade victims to buy non-existent property. Annual cost to victims: $18 million

FBI scammers:
Criminals pretend to be government officials and threaten people who refuse to give them money. Annual cost to victims: $6 million

Phishing:
Criminals pretend to be a real organization, such as a bank, and trick a person into giving them their private information.

Frequency of crimes against Internet users

11,000 attacks every day
458 attacks every hour
8 attacks every minute

Global costs

2015: $450 billion
2020: $4 trillion
Compare to biggest bank robbery in history: $1 billion from Central Bank of Iraq in 2003.

Discussion point

Discuss with a partner.

1 Did any of the statistics surprise you? Why? / Why not?

2 How could you protect yourself from the crimes described?

3 What other types of cybercrime have you heard of?

VIDEO

CRIME DOESN'T PAY

Before you watch

Work with a partner. Discuss the questions.

1 It's said that the modern criminal can steal more with a keyboard than they can with a gun. Do you think this is true? Why? / Why not?

2 How can banks protect themselves from cyber-attacks?

3 What should banks do if they think money has been stolen?

LISTENING 1 Understanding supporting evidence: definitions, examples, and explanations
LISTENING 2 Recognizing citations
STUDY SKILL Being a good listener

VOCABULARY Legal vocabulary
GRAMMAR Verbs for reported speech
SPEAKING Disagreeing politely

Cybercrime.

While you watch

Watch the video. Answer the questions.

1 How did the bank robbers attempt to steal money?

 a in person b online

2 Where did the criminals attempt to transfer money to?

 a An account in Vietnam b An account in Slovenia

3 How much money did they try to steal?

 a 1.36 million dollars b 1.36 million pounds

4 What did the bank do when they noticed a problem?

 a They closed the bank and sent workers home.

 b They stopped the transaction and informed the police.

After you watch

Work with a partner. Discuss the questions.

1 Do you think the criminals "got away with" their crime? Why? / Why not?

2 In the video you hear the expression "Crime doesn't pay." Is this true? Can crime ever pay?

3 How can you protect your bank account from a cyber-attack?

Cybercrime

A Vocabulary preview

1 Match the words in bold with the correct definitions.

1 **Spying** on Internet users is an acceptable way for the police to keep us safe.

2 Finding a way to protect freedom of speech on the Internet is one of the most important **aspects** of cyberlaw.

3 Anyone who is caught trying to break into government computers should face a **severe** fine.

4 A good lawyer will win every **case**.

5 If you're the **victim** of identity theft, your bank should pay back any money that was stolen from you.

6 The best thing to do about online **bullying** is to ignore it, and hope it stops.

7 The Internet makes it too easy to steal other people's **intellectual property**.

8 There need to be stricter controls on what **content** can be shared online.

a (n) a specific part, feature, or quality of something

b (n) behavior that threatens or hurts someone smaller or weaker

c (n) the information or ideas in a book, magazine, movie, website, etc.

d (v) secretly trying to find out information about a person, country, organization, etc.

e (n) an idea, design, or invention that cannot legally be copied or sold

f (n) a matter or situation related to the law, and usually argued in court

g (n) someone who has been harmed, injured, or killed because of a crime or accident

h (adj) very strict or extreme

2 Work with a partner. Discuss the statements. Say if you agree or disagree, and explain your answer.

B Before you listen

Work with a partner. Discuss the questions.

1 What is the meaning of "cyber"? What do you think "cybercrime" means?
2 Have you ever been the victim of cybercrime?
3 What kind of punishments are there for people who download movies illegally?

C Global listening

🎧 **8.1 Listen to a radio show called *Ask an expert*. Number the topics in the order that they are discussed.**

a ___ Cost of cybercrime in 2015
b ___ Examples of crimes that used malware
c ___ Definition of malware
d ___ Punishment for illegal movie downloads
e ___ Definition of computer piracy
f ___ Definition of cybercrime
g ___ Estimated cost of cybercrime in the future
h ___ Definition of intellectual property

Understanding supporting
evidence: definitions,
examples, and explanations

D Close listening

Good speakers use the following to make their ideas clear:

Definitions	This / It is defined as … This / That means …
	X is … X, which means … X, meaning …
Examples	For example, … For instance, …
	To give an / another example, …
	An example of this is … … such as …
Explanations	In other words, … That is to say …
	Specifically, … Let me explain. …

1 🎧 8.1 Listen to *Ask an expert* again, and complete the notes with no more than two words or a number.

CYBERCRIME

Cybercrime *= any [1]_____ committed with a computer.*

(e.g. stealing someone's [2]_____, online bullying, illegal movie downloads, + spying).

Malware *= any kind of [3]_____ used for crime.*

(e.g. stealing [4]_____, spying on users, + unwanted advertising)

Famous cases:

Hackers used malware to break into a White House comp. system in 2014.

Experian website hacked, c [5]_____ million customers had personal info. stolen.

Piracy *= illegally downloading content without [6]_____ for it.*

- *This content = **intellectual property** (sth that sb has created or invented/no one else is legally allowed to make, [7]_____, or sell.)*
- *Punishment for downloading a movie illegally =*
  a) 1 year in jail + $100,000 fine (PERSONAL USE)
  b) 5 years in jail + $250,000 (DOWNLOADING + SELLING).
- *Helen Mirren: "The Internet and piracy will destroy the film industry." (i.e. making movies = [8]_____, and companies will stop if they can't make any money)*

---

2 Look at your answers for Exercise 1, and decide if they are definitions, examples, or explanations.

E Critical thinking

Work in a group. Discuss the questions.

Do you think the punishment for illegally downloading intellectual property is appropriate, too severe, or not severe enough? Why?

Study skills   Being a good listener

Good communication is a two-way process. It requires both good listening skills, and participation in the discussion. You will be a better listener if you make a conscious effort to listen to speakers. Some of these techniques may be useful.

- Consider the speaker's feelings.
- Find ways of encouraging the speaker.
- Focus on the content—think of some way this could be of value to you.
- Listen for key words, and write them down.
- Think of a question you could ask (when the speaker has finished speaking).
- Link what the speaker is saying to something you already know.
- Find one positive comment you could contribute.

© Stella Cottrell (2013)

1 Work with a partner. Discuss which <u>two</u> listening tips would be most useful in each of these situations:

a university lecture	a conversation with a close friend in your 1st language	a conversation with a classmate in English	watching a TV program
a meeting at work	a family discussion	an argument or disagreement	asking for directions or instructions

2 Work with a partner. Discuss the questions.

1 Why are the techniques in the Skills box important?

2 Apart from the situations in Exercise 1, when else are listening skills important?

3 What qualities do you think a good listener needs?

4 Are you a good listener? Why? / Why not?

Protect yourself online

A Vocabulary preview

1 Match the words in bold with the correct definitions.

1	**acquire** (v)	a	actions intended to achieve or deal with something
2	**hack** (v)	b	to illegally break into a computer system in order to steal information
3	**high-tech** (adj)	c	safe from attack, harm, or damage
4	**measures** (n)	d	to get something
5	**motive** (n)	e	the reason you do something
6	**privacy** (n)	f	the most modern or advanced technology available
7	**recover** (v)	g	to get something back that has been lost or stolen
8	**secure** (adj)	h	the freedom to do things without others watching you, or knowing what you're doing

2 Complete the questions with words in bold from Exercise 1.

1 Why do people _____ into government computers?

2 What _____ can you take to protect your personal information online?

3 What can you do to maintain your _____ on social media websites?

4 Why is a _____ Internet connection important when browsing online?

5 What is the main _____ of people who illegally download, and share media for free?

6 What do you think is the easiest way for hackers to _____ your personal information?

7 What steps would you need to take to _____ your identity after theft?

8 Which _____ devices do you think would improve your education?

3 Work with a partner. Discuss the questions in Exercise 2.

B Before you listen

Activating prior knowledge

Work with a partner. Discuss the questions.

1 How can criminals use your computer or cell phone to hurt you?

2 Has a criminal ever "attacked" your computer or cell phone?

3 What are some ways that you can keep your computer and cell phone safe?

C Global listening

 8.2 Listen to *Protect yourself online*. Choose the correct letter, a, b, or c.

1 According to the speaker, the goal of the session is to explain …
   a how to keep your electronic devices safe.
   b how the Federal Trade Commission helps college students.
   c how to prevent identity theft.

2 What is <u>not</u> true about identity theft?
   a It is a type of fraud.
   b It is always a high-tech crime.
   c It can be prevented.

3 To protect personal information …
   a always carry your social security card with you.
   b ask a friend to keep your credit cards for you.
   c never share your information with anyone.

4 Phishing requests come from …
   a criminals.
   b your bank.
   c your credit card company.

5 Which of the following is a strong password?
   a richmondhigh
   b 123456
   c Trustno1

6 To be safe on social media sites, you should …
   a share your mother's maiden name.
   b tell everyone where you were born.
   c check your privacy settings.

7 A student who has been a victim of identity theft should …
   a install anti-virus software on his or her device.
   b inform the police.
   c contact the university computer center.

GLOSSARY

fraud (n) the crime of stealing money by tricking someone

quote (v) to repeat the exact words someone has spoken or written

D Close listening

Quotations from reliable sources are often used to support a speaker's argument. When quoting, speakers have a responsibility to name the original speaker or publisher of the information. This is called *citing the source*. Listeners need to be able to recognize citations in order to know whether information comes from the speaker or an outside source. Study the following examples of citations. Notice the signals that introduce them.

Direct quotation	**Musician Gary Wright said, and I quote,** *"Piracy of music is terrible. It's stealing."*
	In the words of musician Gary Wright, *"Piracy of music is terrible. It's stealing."*
Indirect quotation	**Law professor Robert Braun explained that** *"malware" is a general term for software that's used to commit computer fraud.*
	According to Bill Laberis, *the former editor-in-chief of Computer World, the global cost of cybercrime in 2015 was $500 billion dollars.*

1  8.3 Listen to the first half of *Protect yourself online* again. Complete the quotations with no more than two words.

　1 ＿＿＿＿＿＿ the United States Federal Trade Commission, the agency that's responsible for consumer protection, people between the ages of 18 and 24 are the most likely targets of identity theft.

　2 The United States government ＿＿＿＿＿＿ like this on its website, and I ＿＿＿＿＿＿: "Identity theft is a crime where a thief steals your personal information, such as your full name or your social security number, to commit fraud."

　3 In addition, the well-known consumer protection organization Consumer Reports ＿＿＿＿＿＿ in a 2016 article that identity theft can be either low- or high-tech.

2  8.4 Listen to the second half of *Protect yourself online* again. Match the information (1–3) with the sources (a–c).

　1 Nearly one-fifth of people use the password "123456." ＿＿

　2 Criminals can use information from social media to help them answer security questions for your online accounts. ＿＿

　3 Criminals take advantage of students who share, or trust more than they should on social media. ＿＿

　　a Krystal Merton　　　b Conrad Stewart　　　c Keeper

Critical thinking

Evaluating source reliability

When evaluating the strength of an argument, it's important to think about the source of any information being presented.

In the academic world, the following sources are usually considered reliable: government or university publications; well-regarded magazines such as *Scientific American* or *Consumer Reports*; well-known newspapers like the *New York Times*; and web addresses ending in .gov or .org.

The following sources may not be reliable: websites for commercial products, personal blogs, and non-academic magazines.

To evaluate the reliability of a source, ask yourself these questions:

1   Who wrote or published the information, and what are their qualifications? A reliable source should be a person or publication accepted as an expert in the field.

2   When was the information published? Outdated information is usually not considered reliable.

3   Is the information objective, or is it written with the purpose of trying to persuade people to behave or think in a certain way?

1   🎧 8.5 Listen to extracts from *Cybercrime,* and *Protect yourself online*. Complete the chart with information about the sources.

Source	Qualification	Date published
Bill Laberis, the journal 1_____	former editor-in-chief of the journal *Computer World*	2015
Business Insider	respected magazine	2_____
3_____	(Not given, but reputation is well known)	(Not given)
Federal Trade Commission	US government agency responsible for 4_____	(Not given)
Consumer Reports	well-known consumer protection organization	5_____
Krystal Merton	6_____ at Pennbrook University	(Not given)
Conrad Stewart	Director of 7_____ at the Mayweather Institute in New York.	(Not given)

2   Work in groups. Discuss whether the sources in Exercise 1 are reliable or not.

Vocabulary development

Legal vocabulary

1 Match the words in bold with the correct definitions.

1	**against the law** (adj)	a	the crime of stealing
2	**commit a crime** (v)	b	to do something not allowed by law
3	**criminal offense** (n)	c	money someone is made to pay as a result of a crime
4	**fine** (n)		
5	**legal** (adj)	d	a punishment
6	**penalty** (n)	e	to give a punishment to someone as a result of their crime
7	**sentence** (v)		
8	**theft** (n)	f	not allowed by law
		g	allowed by law
		h	a crime

2 Complete the sentences with words from Exercise 1. Change the form if necessary.

1 Do people use a public library in the area where you live? What is the _____ if you forget to return a book on time?

2 If you park your car illegally in your city, do you have to pay a _____? How much?

3 The police caught a 16-year-old boy trying to steal a car. A judge _____ him to two weeks in jail. It was the boy's first offense. Is that a fair punishment? Why? / Why not?

4 In the United States, and many other places, it is a _____ to talk on a cell phone while driving. Is this law fair, in your opinion?

5 Is it a _____ to throw trash in the street in the place where you live?

6 Have you ever been the victim of _____?

7 Can you think of a situation where a person _____ for a "good" reason?

8 Is it _____ for university students to work in your country? What kind of work can they do?

3 Work with a partner. Discuss the questions in Exercise 2.

Academic words

1 Read the sentences. Match the words in bold with the correct definitions.

1 That's **odd**, I don't think the bank would send you a message on Facebook.

2 I wonder if identity thieves fully **appreciate** the harm they cause their victims.

3 The government **estimates** that the annual cost of fraud could be as high as $50 billion.

4 These emails **expose** Dr. Hartmann as a liar and a criminal.

5 Cyber criminals **exploit** people who are too trusting.

6 If someone is found guilty of identity theft, they may be asked to **compensate** their victims.

a (v) to make something public because you think it's wrong or illegal

b (v) to treat a person unfairly to benefit yourself

c (v) to understand the true nature of something, and why it is important

d (v) to pay someone money because they have suffered injury or loss

e (v) to guess the amount or value of something

f (adj) strange or unusual

2 Work with a partner. Discuss the questions.

1 Have you ever received an odd email from a company asking for personal information?

2 How can you make other students fully appreciate the dangers of cybercrime?

3 It is estimated that children are 35% more likely to be the target of identity theft than adults. Does this surprise you? Why? / Why not?

4 Is it ever acceptable for hackers to expose information to the public?

5 Has anyone you know ever been exploited by a cyber-criminal? What happened?

6 Who do you think should compensate you if you're a victim of identity theft: your bank or the criminals themselves? Why?

Speaking model

You are going to learn about reporting verbs, disagreeing politely, and using word stress to strongly agree or disagree. You are then going to use these to have a debate about illegal movie downloads.

A Analyze

Read the model and answer the questions below.

> **Jenny:** Could someone review the case for me? What was it about?
>
> **Luis:** OK, so this student who was failing several courses hacked into the university database, and changed three of his grades from Fs to As. However, he made a mistake, and university staff were able to connect the break-in to his account. He was arrested, and sentenced to 200 hours of community service. He was also kicked out of the university.
>
> **Felicity:** I think the sentence was much too light. At his trial, he admitted knowing it was wrong to hack into the database. He even said, and I quote, "It was easier to change my grades than to go to class, and work hard." I think he should have been sentenced to at least six months in jail, plus a fine.
>
> **Al:** I understand what you're saying, but I disagree with you about the sentence. He was only 18 years old. It was his first semester, and he was having a lot of trouble adjusting to college. Plus, he was under a lot of pressure from his parents to do well. I know, that's not an excuse for hacking, but it shows the kind of stress he was under. I strongly believe jail is the wrong punishment for this type of crime. Community service seems about right. He could spend that time teaching kids, and senior citizens how to use computers – legally!

1 What was the student's crime? What reason did he give?

2 What punishment did the student receive?

3 What is Felicity's opinion of the punishment? What reason does she give?

4 Why does Al say, *"I understand what you're saying …"* before disagreeing?

B Discuss

Work with a partner. Discuss the questions.

1 Do you agree that the student's action should be a criminal offense?

2 Do you think the punishment was too strict, too light, or correct?

3 Should the student receive a lighter punishment because of his age, and personal situation?

Grammar

Verbs for reported speech

The verb you use in reported speech can make your statements more interesting, precise, or forceful. For example:

*Professor Roberts **insisted** that movie piracy actually seems to increase sales.*

*The actress **warned** that illegal downloads could seriously damage the movie industry.*

verb + (*that*)

admit, argue, claim, comment, complain, demand, deny, estimate, insist, observe, remark, report, reveal, state, suggest

verb + object + (*that*)

advise, assure, promise, inform

verb + object + *to* + base form

advise, encourage, expect, instruct, warn

verb + *-ing*

deny, propose, recommend, report

1 Choose the correct reporting verb to complete each sentence.

1 Tom Walker was sentenced to 10 years in prison after he **admitted / demanded** downloading and selling 10,000 songs illegally.

2 The lawyer **argued / boasted** that his client should go free.

3 The security expert **instructed / promised** the audience to make sure their anti-virus software is always up to date.

4 The student **expected / denied** attempting to hack into the website.

5 The company spokesman **requested / revealed** that hackers had broken into the computer system, and stolen more than 20,000 user IDs.

2 Rewrite the quotations in reported speech using the verb in parentheses.

1 The Internet security website Norton said, "Somebody's identity is stolen every three seconds as a result of cybercrime." (report)

2 The chief of police told the audience, "My department is working on reducing cybercrime in the area." (assure)

3 A leading technology expert recently said, "Cybercrime is rising year on year." (state)

4 Three years ago, the *Wall Street Journal* informed readers, "The estimated cost of cybercrime in the U.S. is approximately $100 billion." (reveal)

Speaking skill

It can be challenging to express your opinion politely when you disagree with someone. The best way to do this is to "soften" your opinion using one of the following techniques.

a Acknowledge the other speaker's point of view, and make it clear that you understand it. Then state your own position:

I see what you're saying, but I think fines for piracy should be stricter.

b Acknowledge that your opinion is yours alone, and other people may disagree:

It seems to me that the level of punishment doesn't match the crime.

c Pretend to be unsure of your opinion:

I'm not sure I agree with the judge in this case.

d Hedge—use words like *may, might, could, supposedly, perhaps, maybe*— to make your opinion sound less forceful.

I believe that tough sentences may actually prevent crime.

1 Work with a partner. Match the sentences (1–6) with a technique (a–d) from the Skills box.

   1 ___ "I understand what you're saying, but he broke the law. He deserves to be punished."

   2 ___ "I don't know if I agree with what you're saying."

   3 ___ "I suppose you could say that, but he didn't actually hurt anyone."

   4 ___ "For me, anyone who breaks the law should expect punishment."

   5 ___ "Personally, I don't believe a three-year sentence is enough."

   6 ___ "Perhaps the punishment for downloading just one movie shouldn't have been so severe ."

2 Work with a partner. Take turns reading the statements. Use a variety of expressions from the Skills box to disagree politely with your partner.

   1 "Textbooks are too expensive. I think it's fine to photocopy books to save money."

   2 "Why should I pay for a song if I can download a pirated copy, and listen to it for free?"

   3 "I know it's illegal to download movies without paying, but it's not really hurting anybody, is it?"

   4 "A sentence of one year in jail is too short for illegal movie downloads."

   5 "A sentence of five years is too long for illegal movie downloads."

   6 "The best way to prevent piracy is to make all movies and songs free."

Pronunciation for speaking

Using word stress to strongly agree or disagree

English speakers use a variety of adverbs to express strong agreement or disagreement with something a speaker says. These include: *strongly, completely, totally, absolutely, really, entirely.*

Speakers use a "rising-falling" intonation pattern in sentences that express strong opinion. Typically, the speaker's voice rises to its highest point on the stressed syllable of the adverb. The voice then falls on the word that follows. For example:

*Most Americans **strong**ly support free public education.*

1 🎧 8.6 Read the sentences below. Underline the stressed syllable in each adverb, and draw an arrow to show the "rising-falling" intonation pattern. Then listen and check.

1 I completely agree with you; the punishment doesn't match the crime.

2 You're absolutely right. Young people don't understand that this is a serious crime.

3 I totally disagree. She broke the law, and deserves to be punished.

4 I strongly disagree with sending people to prison for Internet fraud.

5 I really don't think that's true. Downloading something without permission is a crime.

2 Work with a partner. Read and discuss the case studies. Student A: say what you think the punishment should be. Student B: agree or disagree strongly using an adverb, and the "rising-falling" stress pattern.

1 A "cyber-gang" hacked into the computer system of a nationwide chain store. They stole the names, credit card numbers, and personal information of over 150,000 customers. One member of the gang was caught, and found guilty. What should his punishment be?

2 A student hacked into a university database containing thousands of student papers. The student downloaded dozens of papers. Later he copied one of the papers, and submitted it in one of his classes. The student was caught when the professor recognized the paper. What crimes did the student commit? What should his punishment be?

3 A woman was arrested after sending out more than 10,000 phishing emails designed to trick senior citizens into giving her their bank details. Using the information she received, the woman was able to steal more than $200,000 from innocent victims. The judge sentenced the woman to 15 years in a jail, and a $250,000 fine. Was this a fair sentence?

Speaking task

Debate the appropriacy of a punishment in a cybercrime case study.

Brainstorm

Work in groups of four. Read the case study and answer the questions.

Early last year, university student Sean Thomas, 19, was found guilty of copyright infringement for downloading and distributing more than 150 movies via the illegal sharing site Aperture. Thomas was fined $185,000, and sentenced to three years in prison. In a statement to the press Thomas said, "I can't believe this is happening. Everyone I know downloads music, movies, and TV shows all the time. Some of them have multiple hard drives full of illegal content. All I did was download a few movies. Just for that my life is ruined." When asked whether or not the sentence given Thomas had been too strict, Judge Nina Williamson said, "Young people today don't think about the consequences of their actions. They need to understand that downloading a movie without permission from the company that owns it is illegal. It is stealing, plain and simple. Let this case be a warning that anyone caught doing so in this state will face severe punishment."

1   What crime did Sean Thomas commit?
2   What punishment was he given?
3   What reason did the judge give for the sentence?

Plan

Divide your group of four students into two pairs.

You will debate the following statement: *Sean Thomas broke the law. The punishment he received was appropriate to the level of his crime.*

Pair 1: You agree with the statement above.

Pair 2: You disagree with the statement above. With your partner, make a list of four or five ideas to support your position. Turn to page 188 to find quotations that support your arguments.

Speak

Hold your debate. Think about your language and tone when you agree or disagree.

Share

Choose one student from each group to present the results of the debate to the class. The speaker should summarize the main ideas that each side used to support its position.

Reflect

With a partner, discuss the most effective way to deal with illegal movie downloads. Explain your reasoning.

Review

Wordlist

MACMILLAN
DICTIONARY

Vocabulary preview

acquire (v) **	high-tech (adj) **	secure (adj) **
aspect (n) ***	intellectual property (n)	severe (adj) ***
bullying (n)	measure (n) ***	spying (n)
case (n) ***	motive (n) **	victim (n) ***
content (n) ***	privacy (n) *	
hack (v) *	recover (v) ***	

Vocabulary development

against the law (phr)	fine (n) ***	sentence (v) ***
commit a crime (phr)	legal (adj) ***	theft (n) **
criminal offense (n)	penalty (n) ***	

Academic words

appreciate (adj) **	estimate (v) ***	expose (v) **
compensate (v) **	exploit (v) **	odd (adj) ***

Academic words review

Complete the sentences using words from the box.

estimated exposes exploit incidence sequence

1   Managers must be careful not to _____ their staff if they want to have good working relationships.

2   Since the Ebola epidemic, health workers have managed to reduce the _____ of the disease in West Africa.

3   We don't really know what happened. The _____ of events isn't clear.

4   It's _____ that the new process will save over $400 million dollars a year.

5   The review _____ serious issues with the research methodology.

Unit review

Listening 1 ☐ I can understand different types of supporting evidence.

Listening 2 ☐ I can listen for quotations and citations.

Study skill ☐ I can be a good listener.

Vocabulary ☐ I can use legal vocabulary.

Grammar ☐ I can use reporting verbs.

Speaking ☐ I can disagree politely.

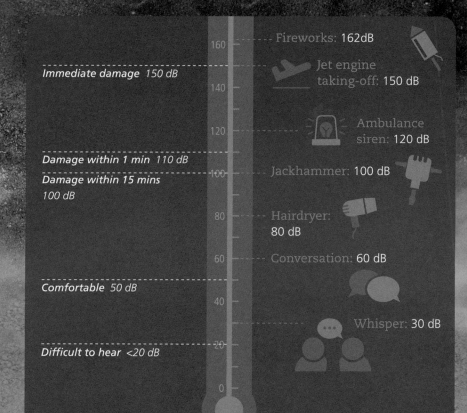

Noise thermometer

Discussion point

Discuss with a partner.

1 In a typical day, how many of the sounds in the infographic are you exposed to?

2 Based on this information, which kind of jobs are potentially harmful to your hearing?

3 Where do you think the following sounds would fit on the infographic: a vacuum cleaner, a crying baby, and a refrigerator?

Immediate damage 150 dB

Damage within 1 min 110 dB

Damage within 15 mins 100 dB

Comfortable 50 dB

Difficult to hear <20 dB

160
140
120
100
80
60
40
20
0

Fireworks: 162dB

Jet engine taking-off: 150 dB

Ambulance siren: 120 dB

Jackhammer: 100 dB

Hairdryer: 80 dB

Conversation: 60 dB

Whisper: 30 dB

VIDEO

UNDER THE FLIGHT PATH

Before you watch

Work with a partner. Discuss the questions.

1 Would you like to live near an airport? Why? / Why not?

2 How could living near an airport have a negative effect on your health?

3 Which do you think is worse for your health: living near an airport or smoking? Why?

UNIT AIMS

LISTENING 1 Listening for organization
LISTENING 2 Listening to interpret the speaker's attitude
STUDY SKILL Plagiarism

VOCABULARY Word + preposition combinations
GRAMMAR Cleft sentences
SPEAKING Fielding questions during a presentation

Inner-city construction.

While you watch

Watch the video. Choose *T* (True) or *F* (False).

1   The study looked at 3.6 million people
    living near Heathrow airport.   T / F

2   People living near the airport have a 10 to 20%
    decreased risk of heart disease and strokes.   T / F

3   Some people can't sleep because
    they're stressed out by the noise.   T / F

4   The residents interviewed in the video
    all complained about the noise.   T / F

5   Smoking has a greater impact on
    your health than noise pollution.   T / F

After you watch

Work with a partner. Discuss the questions.

1   The study showed a correlation between living
    near the airport and an increased risk of heart
    disease. However, this doesn't mean one *causes*
    the other. What other factors might have caused
    the increased risk?

2   What can airline companies do to reduce noise
    pollution?

1 LISTENING

That's so annoying!

A Vocabulary preview

1 Match the words in bold with the correct definitions.

1 The students were so **distracted** by the construction noise that they didn't do as well as expected on their exam.

a   unable to concentrate   b   fearful of

2 The **distant** car alarm was so loud it seemed like it was nearby.

a   far away   b   unusual

3 Some people are better at blocking out **repetitive** noises than others.

a   happening occasionally   b   happening again and again

4 The noise from the stadium **irritated** the families that wanted to sleep.

a   excited   b   annoyed

5 **Initially**, the sound didn't bother us. After a few hours, it did though.

a   at first   b   slowly

6 The sound was **unpredictable**. No one knew when it would start or stop.

a   changing slowly   b   changing in unexpected ways

7 Most people are **sensitive to** loud sounds, and try to avoid them.

a   have an interest in   b   feel the effect strongly

8 The bell continued ringing. The students wondered when it would **cease.**

a   stop completely   b   increase slowly

2 Complete the sentences using the words in bold from Exercise 1.

1 I'm beginning to get a little _____ by that car alarm.

2 I don't like working at home. It's too easy to get _____.

3 _____, we enjoyed waking up to birdsong, but it soon became annoying.

4 Dogs are more _____ high-frequency sounds than people are.

5 At night I can hear the _____ noise of traffic on the freeway.

6 Car alarms are really annoying. I think it's because they're so _____.

7 Lightning is _____, which is one of the things that makes it so dangerous.

8 The company was forced to _____ construction after locals complained about noise levels.

A buzzing mosquito

B Before you listen

Work with a partner. Discuss which of these sounds annoy you.

a plane flying overhead	a smoke alarm
a baby crying	bird song
a dentist's drill	someone eating
a dog barking	fingernails on a chalkboard
a mosquito buzzing	someone snoring

C Global listening

There are many ways a speaker may let you know how the information you are about to hear will be organized. For example:

We'll focus on four reasons for …

Let's consider three factors …

Two examples of this are …

These number-signal phrases tell you what to listen for. Use them to help you follow the ideas you hear, and to organize your notes.

GLOSSARY

frequency (n) the rate at which a sound, light, or radio wave repeats

pitch (n) the high or low quality of a sound

🎧 **9.1** Listen to *That's so annoying!* Number the topics in the order they are presented.

___ The irregular flight patterns of insects

___ Nails on a chalkboard

___ The role of how long a sound lasts

___ Reasons repetitive sounds are annoying

___ The frequency of the sound as a factor

D Close listening

🎧 **9.1** Listen to *That's so annoying!* again. Choose the correct letters, a, b, or c, to answer the questions.

1 Why are strangers' cell phone calls annoying?

    a   They are often very loud.

    b   We don't want to know about their personal lives.

    c   We don't know when they will end.

2 What is a dripping faucet given as an example of?

    a   A noise that is high frequency.

    b   A noise that is repetitive.

    c   A noise that is unpredictable.

3 What does the interviewer mean when he says the sound of his dripping faucet seems to "magnify in strength"?

    a   It seems to get quieter.

    b   It seems to get louder.

    c   It seems to change pitch.

4 Why is it impossible to predict how loud a mosquito will sound to us?

    a   They fly in irregular patterns.

    b   They often fly next to our ear.

    c   The pitch of the sound is constantly changing.

5 Why are fingernails on a chalkboard annoying?

    a   The sound is continuous.

    b   The sound is unpredictable.

    c   The sound is high-pitched.

E Critical thinking

Work in a group. Discuss the questions.

1 Apart from the three factors given in the podcast, what else makes a sound annoying? Give examples.

2 Do you believe that noise causes stress? Why? / Why not?

3 What practical steps could be taken to reduce noise levels in cities?

Study skills   Plagiarism

What is plagiarism?

Plagiarism means using someone else's work without acknowledging that it was the source of information or inspiration. It is treated very seriously, and plagiarized work is usually disqualified. This can have a major impact on your marks or grades.

How to avoid plagiarism

- Write all notes in your own words.
- Write down exactly where you read the information you put in your notes.
- Make it clear when you're using a direct quotation—copy words *exactly*, use "quotation marks," and state the source.

© Stella Cottrell (2013)

1   Read the following extract from *That's so annoying!*

> *"First, a sound can be annoying because we don't know when it will stop. The question of how long the sound will last is what upsets us. Even a distant bell or quiet beep can have this effect. At first you may not notice the sound. But, if it continues, it becomes distracting—and increasingly annoying. … For example, the common experience of being irritated by a stranger's phone conversation in a public place. … Initially, you may hardly notice the conversation. As the conversation continues, however, you start to feel slightly annoyed. You may tell yourself it's because the person is speaking too loudly; or because you don't want to know a stranger's personal details. My research, however, has revealed it's not knowing when the conversation will end that makes it so annoying."*

2   Summarize the text in your own words in your notebook.

3   Work with a partner. Use the questions below to assess your partner's summary.

   1   Is any of the summary copied directly from the text above?
   2   Are any quotes included? If so, do they follow the rules in the Study skills box?
   3   Does the summary accurately explain the main ideas in the original text?

Was that my phone ringing?

A Vocabulary preview

1 Match the words in bold with the correct definitions.

1	**anticipate** (v)	a	nervously
2	**anxiously** (adv)	b	to be aware or conscious of something
3	**make sense of** (phr v)	c	to cause something to begin
4	**perceive** (v)	d	difference in level or amount
5	**prompt** (v)	e	to expect something to happen
6	**recall** (v)	f	to understand, to get the meaning from
7	**tie in with** (phr v)	g	to be connected to
8	**variation** (n)	h	to remember something

2 Complete the sentences with words from Exercise 1. Change the form if necessary.

1 Studies suggest listening to music increases our ability to _____ information.

2 They waited _____ for a call from the hospital.

3 This makes it difficult to _____ when we'll hear the sound next.

4 Plans to build a new airport have _____ concerns about noise pollution.

5 _____ in temperature can affect the pitch of a musical instrument.

6 Only one of the test subjects was able to _____ the low-frequency sounds.

7 This _____ the idea that high noise levels can cause stress.

8 Our brains work hard to _____ what we hear.

3 Work with a partner. Discuss the questions.

1 When was the last time you waited anxiously for a call?

2 Do you think we perceive sounds differently as we get older?

3 Why do you think it's easier to recall song lyrics than historical dates?

B Before you listen

Activating prior knowledge

Work with a partner. Discuss the questions.

1 Have you ever woken up in the night, and felt like you couldn't move?

2 Have you ever heard a sound in a dream, and thought it was real?

3 Have you ever been in a crowd, and felt sure you heard someone call your name, but no one actually did?

C Global listening

1 🎧 9.2 Listen to *Was that my phone ringing?* Answer the questions.

1 How is a phantom phone ring defined by the speaker?

a A call made by a stranger.

b A call that doesn't occur.

c A call that is unexpected.

2 Which of the following is given as a possible cause of phantom phone rings?

a depression

b stress

c boredom

3 What might phantom vibrations be caused by?

a The brain perceiving sounds.

b The brain overpredicting.

c The brain confusing sounds.

4 According to the podcast, why do Chinese students hear Chinese words?

a The brain prefers to hear Chinese.

b The brain processes information.

c The brain tries to make meaning.

5 What is the focus of the podcast?

a The causes of phone vibrations.

b How humans wait for calls.

c Reasons the brain plays tricks.

2 Work with a partner. Summarize the main reason why people hear phantom sounds.

Listening to interpret the speaker's attitude

D Close listening

As you listen, pay attention to the descriptive words the speaker uses to present ideas, and details. This will help you understand not only the facts presented, but the speaker's attitude toward the information. For example:

A stranger variation …

Interestingly, …

That isn't likely, …

It seems strange, …

Perhaps ….

After you finish listening, review the details you understood. Ask yourself how the various ideas are connected, and what the speaker's attitude is toward them.

1  9.2 Listen to *Was that my phone ringing?* again. Choose *T* (True) or *F* (False).

1 The speaker thinks phantom phone rings are a curious phenomenon.   T / F

2 The speaker doesn't think smartphones affect phantom phone rings.   T / F

3 The speaker believes our anticipation of a call may cause phantom rings.   T / F

4 The speaker thinks phantom vibrations are an annoying phenomenon. T / F

5 The speaker isn't surprised that volunteers in the first study heard phantom words.   T / F

6 The speaker thinks the most interesting aspect of the second study is that learners thought words had been added to the recordings.   T / F

2 Work with a partner. Correct the false statements in Exercise 1.

E Critical thinking

Work with a partner. Discuss the questions.

1 Why do you think the language learners experienced phantom words in the study? Have you experienced these while listening to English? Describe what you heard.

2 Life in the modern world, especially in large cities, is filled with a variety of sounds. How does this compare to 100 years ago? How would it have been different?

Critical thinking

Moving the goalposts

"Moving the goalposts" means changing the rules or conditions of something to make it harder for someone else to succeed. For example, imagine you're taking part in a debate, and your opponent makes a claim that you can prove isn't true. However, when you present them with the evidence, they won't admit you're right. Instead, they claim you don't have enough evidence, or the right kind of evidence, and ask for something different.

This is a common technique used by speakers who feel they're losing a discussion or a debate, or are simply determined not to change their minds.

1 Work with a partner. Read the extract and answer the questions.

Alan Webber: There is simply no evidence to suggest aircraft noise has a negative effect on your health.

Interviewer: Actually, a recent study of people living near Heathrow airport suggests those that exposed to high levels of aircraft noise are 10–20% more likely to be admitted to hospital for heart disease.

Alan Webber: Well, that was only a small study. We need more research.

Interviewer: The study looked at 3.6 million residents living near the airport. I wouldn't call that small. Would you?

Alan Webber: Ah, but this study only looked at one airport in the U.K. What about other countries? If this were a real issue, international research would support it.

Interviewer: International research does seem to support it. A 2009 study of 6 million residents living near 89 different American airports showed that those aged over 65 were at higher risk of heart disease.

Alan Webber: Yes, well that's just their age, isn't it? It's nothing to do with aircraft noise …

1 Which speaker "moves the goalposts"?

2 How many times does he do this? Underline the examples.

3 Why do you think he does this?

4 Do you think the interviewer reacts well to this? Why? / Why not?

2 Work in a group. Discuss the questions.

1 Do you think this is an effective way to argue? Why? / Why not?

2 In a debate, is it acceptable to change your opinion if evidence suggests you're wrong? Why? / Why not?

Vocabulary development

> ## Word + preposition combinations
>
> In English, many adjectives, verbs, and nouns are often followed by a specific preposition (sometimes called a "dependent preposition"). Some examples are:
>
> <u>Adjective + preposition</u>
>
> *You may be **unaware of** the research results.*
>
> <u>Verb + preposition</u>
>
> *Can you **relate to** what I'm saying?*
>
> <u>Noun + preposition</u>
>
> *There has been an **increase in** noise pollution in recent years.*

1 🎧 9.3 Complete the text with the prepositions in the box. Then listen and check.

> by   from (x4)   of   on   to (x2)   with

Noise in cities can **interfere** [1]_____ normal activities such as sleeping. It can disrupt the quality [2]_____ **life**. It is difficult to **escape** [3]_____ sounds in a city. A lot of the outdoor noise, the environmental noise, in cities is **caused** [4]_____ transportation. Cars, taxis, buses, trains, and subways all cause noise pollution. People adapt to noise, but face health problems **due** [5]_____ noise levels. One problem is hearing loss. When people hear loud noises regularly, this **contributes** [6]_____ hearing loss. Some people also **suffer** [7]_____ high stress levels. City planners are beginning to understand that they need to create parks for their citizens in them. A well-planned park provides a quiet space for people to relax, and **get away** [8]_____ noise. Because noise seems to have an **impact** [9]_____ animals, they also **benefit** [10]_____ having parks to enjoy.

2 Correct the mistakes in each sentence.

1 If students are distracted from noise during their exams, this can lead to poor exam results.

2 Because noise pollution is a problem in big cities, it's vital for people's health to be able to escape with the noise.

3 Researchers are aware of the impact of noise to people's stress levels.

4 We are more irritated from low sounds because our ears are sensitive to them.

5 If the design in a park appeals with many people, they will go there frequently to enjoy it.

6 Many people suffer of hearing loss due from the sounds they are exposed to at work.

Academic words

1 Complete the definitions with the words in bold.

1 Studies suggest that overhearing conversations is more distracting than **random** noises.

2 The researchers **obtained** some surprising results from their experiment.

3 One study **revealed** a possible link between aircraft noise and higher blood pressure.

4 There are many ways to analyze and **interpret** scientific data.

5 The researchers **concluded** that low-level noise can negatively affect sleep cycles.

6 The study seems to **presume** we're all exposed to the same level of noise at night.

a (v) to let something become known

b (v) to explain or decide the meaning of something

c (v) to decide something is true after looking at all the evidence

d (v) to get something, often after a long process

e (v) to think something is true because it's likely, even if you are not certain

f (adj) happening without a particular method or purpose

2 Complete the sentences with words from Exercise 1. Change the form if necessary.

1 We _____ results from a 2015 report suggesting that reducing dangerous noise levels could save the U.S. $3.9 billion a year.

2 A recent study _____ that people who live near airports are more likely to suffer from heart disease.

3 A 2013 review has led scientists _____ that the general public are exposed to fewer high-frequency sounds now than in the past.

4 Japanese researchers found that work-related discussions are less distracting than _____ noises in the workplace.

5 Playing a musical instrument badly affects your ability _____ people's emotions, a study suggests.

6 Although we often _____ that listening to loud music on headphones damages hearing, recent research suggests there isn't enough evidence to support this conclusion.

3 Work with a partner. Which of the sentences in Exercise 2 do you think are true? Explain your reasons.

Speaking model

You are going to learn about cleft sentences, fielding questions during a presentation, and using contrastive stress for emphasis. You are then going to use these to help you plan, and present a design for a city park.

A Analyze

Jay:	Hi, everyone. We've decided to address the issue of noise pollution in the university library. First, we will present a summary of the problems we have identified. Then we will talk about ways to eliminate these issues, and provide a better study space for students.
	The first issue we've identified is students talking. Even if they talk quietly, it seems to disturb other students. Another issue is the use of cell phones. The biggest problem here is the loud noise they make every time someone receives an email or text message. Also, some students think it's acceptable to take calls. Finally, the library is incredibly popular, and such a large number of people coming and going can make a lot of noise.
	So, how do we propose to resolve these issues? First, create group study rooms where students can quietly talk together. Second, prohibit cell phones. Students in the library should be studying, not socializing! Finally, keep the library open 24 hours a day. This will make the library less crowded, and therefore less noisy. Are there any questions?
Eve:	You said that people taking calls was the biggest issue with cell phones, but couldn't those students just go outside? You don't need to ban cell phones completely!
Jayne:	Actually, it's the loud noise phones make when you receive a message that seems to be the biggest problem. But yes, I suppose people could go outside to take calls. Is anything else unclear?
Carla:	I can't see where the group study rooms are in your design …

Work with a partner. Read the model and answer the questions.

1 What problems did the group identify?
2 What is their solution for each problem?
3 Which phrase does Jay use to correct Eve?
4 What phrases does the speaker use to invite listeners to ask questions?

B Discuss

With a partner, discuss whether you think Jay's solutions will work or not. Explain your reasoning.

Grammar

Cleft sentences

In conversation you can highlight information you want someone to focus on by dividing a sentence into two clauses instead of one. This is called a **cleft sentence**.

Regular form	Cleft form
	It + be + relative clause
Stress makes you hear the phantom ring.	It's stress that makes you hear the phantom ring.
Shin kept hearing the sound.	It was Shin who kept hearing the sound.

Note we often use this form to correct wrong information:

A: I'm just doing some revision for the exam on Wednesday.

B: It's Tuesday we have the exam, not Wednesday.

1   Work with a partner. Underline the cleft sentences then practice the conversations.

1   A: It's the constant drip, drip, drip of that faucet that's bothering me.

    B: I know. It really distracts me when I'm trying to study.

2   A: Did Amin say he would meet us at the library?

    B: No, it was at the science center.

3   A: Hey, is the guest lecturer coming this Tuesday?

    B: No, it's next Tuesday she's coming.

4   A: I'm worried about the grammar section of the exam.

    B: It's the reading section that's difficult for me.

2   Work with a partner. Roleplay conversations using cleft constructions and your own ideas.

1   A: Was that your phone ringing? That's an unusual ring tone.

    B: It was … [say another sound] you heard. My phone is on vibrate.

2   A: Did you hear that car alarm during our exam? I couldn't concentrate at all.

    B: It was … [Say another sound was more annoying and explain why.]

3   A: I didn't see Ali in class on Monday. Maybe because of the storm.

    B: [Confirm Ali wasn't in class, and explain why the storm caused his absence.]

Speaking skill

After a presentation, it's common to give listeners the opportunity to ask questions:

Are there any questions?   *Is anything unclear?*

Did you understand everything about …?

It's also common to repeat questions you are asked. This helps confirm you've understood the questions correctly, makes sure everyone else has heard the questions, and gives you a chance to think of an answer:

You asked what I meant by …   *The question was … [repeat the question].*

Often, we need clarify what we've said by giving follow-up information:

That's a good question.   *Let me explain / give you an example …*

1 🎧 9.4 Listen and complete the conversations with no more than four words.

   1 A: OK, _____ questions?

      B: Yes, what is "pitch"?

      A: _____: what is pitch? Pitch means how high or low a sound is.

   2 A: What sound did you say is the most annoying?

      B: You _____ what sound I said is the most annoying, correct?

   3 A: Do some sounds become less annoying if we hear them every day?

      B: That's _____. I'm not sure.

   4 A: That's all the information we gathered. _____ what I said about our group's conclusion?

      B: Not exactly.

2 Choose one of the topics below. Prepare a one- to two-minute presentation. Take notes on the points you will cover.

   1 Describe a sound that annoys you.

      What is the sound?   Why does it annoy you?

      Where do you hear it?

   2 Describe a piece of music that is important to you.

      What kind of music is it?   How does it make you feel?

      Why is it important to you?

   3 Describe a place that has a problem with noise pollution.

      Where is it?   How do you think this issue could be solved?

      What causes the noise pollution?

3 Work in groups. Give your presentations then field questions from the group.

Pronunciation for speaking

> ## Using contrastive stress for emphasis
>
> English has regular stress patterns. The most important content words are stressed in a sentence. You can emphasize an idea by shifting the stress from the regular stress pattern. You can do this in different ways depending on what you want to focus on:
>
> *Our **ears** don't identify the sounds we hear, our brains do.* (To emphasize what <u>doesn't</u> identify the sounds.)
>
> *Our ears don't identify the sounds we hear, our **brains** do.* (To emphasize what <u>does</u> identify the sounds.)

1 🎧 9.5 Listen to the sentences. Underline the contrasted words. Practice with a partner.

  1 Low sounds actually affect us more than high sounds.

  2 Hassan imagined the phone rang because he wanted it to ring.

  3 Elliott complained about the noise, but it didn't bother Jude.

  4 Fireworks are louder than jet engines.

  5 Aida heard so many phantom rings that she ignored a real call.

2 🎧 9.6 Listen and match the sentences (1–4) with their meanings (a–d).

Sentence 1	a Lara's is worse, though.
Sentence 2	b His old ringtone wasn't quite as bad.
Sentence 3	c It didn't affect the rest of her family.
Sentence 4	d At night it wasn't as loud.

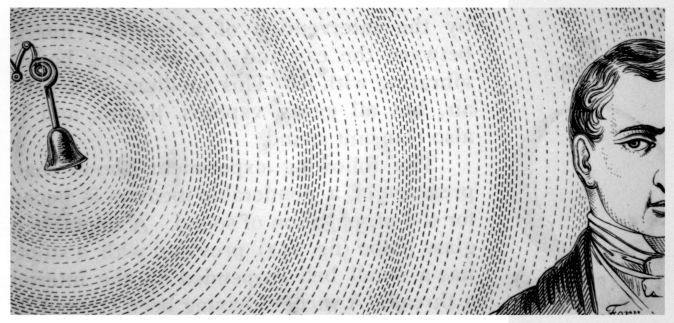

Speaking task

Design and present a park that allows people to escape noise pollution in the city.

Brainstorm

Imagine your group is going to plan a park where people can relax, and enjoy pleasant sounds. Compile lists of noise pollution problems in cities, and pleasant sounds you think are important for people to hear. List at least four ideas in each category.

Problems	Pleasant sounds

Plan

Plan a presentation on a park design you think would take into consideration different age groups, and the types of activities they enjoy. Follow these steps:

1   Organize a summary of the urban noise problems you've identified.
2   Make notes on how the park would be designed to eliminate noise issues, and provide a relaxing space. For each feature, include enough details to make your plan clear to your audience.
3   Make a simple drawing to explain the design of the park.

Features in the park	Details of each feature

Speak

Present your plan to other groups. Pause to field questions, and to explain any ideas someone tells you are unclear. Remember to use cleft sentences, and contrastive word stress for emphasis.

Share

Return to your group. Compare the ideas that other groups had. Then share your conclusions about what would be a successful urban space.

Reflect

Work with a partner. Discuss the questions.

1   In some countries, using cell phones on public transportation is prohibited during rush hour. Do you think this is a good idea? Why? / Why not?
2   Have you ever suffered from "phantom vibration syndrome"?
3   What steps can be taken to reduce noise pollution in cities?

Review

Wordlist

MACMILLAN
DICTIONARY

Vocabulary preview

anticipate (v) **	distracted (adj)	perceive (v) **	sensitive to (adj) ***
anxiously (adv)	initially (adv) ***	prompt (v) **	ties in with (phr v)
cease (v) **	irritated (adj)	recall (v) ***	unpredictable (adj) *
distant (adj) **	make sense of (phr)	repetitive (adj)	variation (n) ***

Vocabulary development

benefit from (v + prep) ***	contribute to (v + prep) ***	escape from (v + prep) ***	interfere with (v + prep)
caused by (v + prep) ***	due to (adj + prep) ***	get away with (phr v)	quality of life (n)
		impact on (n) ***	suffer from (v + prep) ***

Academic words

conclude (v) ***	obtain (v) ***	random (adj) **
interpret (v) ***	presume (v) *	reveal (v) ***

Academic words review

Complete the sentences using words from the box.

economy	presume	random	revenue	visible

1 Competing athletes have to take _____ drug tests in an attempt to stamp out doping in sport.

2 Some economists think the UK's _____ will suffer when it leaves the EU.

3 The pyramids are _____ from the top floor of our hotel.

4 Our software development business is expected to generate a _____ of $4 million this year.

5 "I _____ you've already booked your flight for the 14th?".

Unit review

Listening 1		I can listen for organization.
Listening 2		I can interpret a speaker's attitude.
Study skill		I know how to avoid plagiarism.
Vocabulary		I can use word + preposition combinations.
Grammar		I can use cleft sentences.
Speaking		I can field questions during a presentation.

SOUND UNIT 9 169

Discussion point

Discuss with a partner.

1 Which predictions from the infographic are most likely to come true?

2 Which changes will have the biggest impact on the way we travel in the future?

3 What other predictions can you make about the future of transportation?

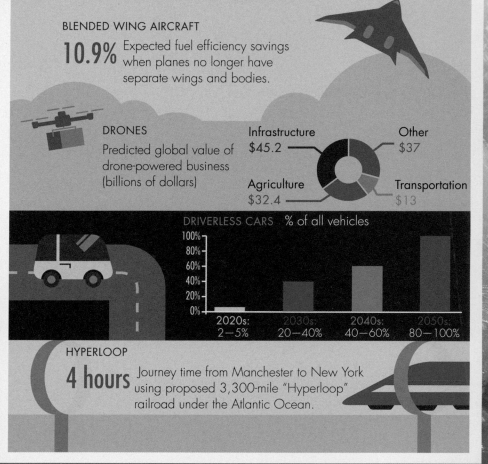

THE **FUTURE** OF TRANSPORTATION

BLENDED WING AIRCRAFT

10.9% Expected fuel efficiency savings when planes no longer have separate wings and bodies.

DRONES
Predicted global value of drone-powered business (billions of dollars)

Infrastructure $45.2

Other $37

Agriculture $32.4

Transportation $13

DRIVERLESS CARS   % of all vehicles

	2020s: 2–5%	2030s: 20–40%	2040s: 40–60%	2050s: 80–100%

HYPERLOOP

4 hours Journey time from Manchester to New York using proposed 3,300-mile "Hyperloop" railroad under the Atlantic Ocean.

VIDEO

BAT-WING DRONES

Before you watch

1 **Work with a partner. Discuss whether the following sentences are *T* (True) or *F* (False).**

1 Drones are remote-controlled.   T / F

2 Drones normally look like helicopters.   T / F

3 Drones are only used for flying as hobbies.   T / F

2 **Watch the video and check your answers.**

UNIT
AIMS

LISTENING 1 Listening for bias
LISTENING 2 Listening for hyperbole
STUDY SKILL Planning a persuasive argument

VOCABULARY Transportation and logistics
GRAMMAR Future perfect progressive
SPEAKING Language for convincing and making persuasive arguments

Delivery drones.

While you watch

Watch the video and put the topics in the order they're mentioned.

____ The drone in the video was inspired by how a bat flies.

____ The bat-wing design will make the drone fly over water and fly for longer.

____ Bats' wings change shape and will make the drone fly more efficiently.

____ Drones are becoming more popular than traditional remote-controlled airplanes.

____ The wings of the drone inflate and work like a hovercraft when it takes off.

After you watch

Work with a partner. Discuss the questions.

1 Would you ever like to fly a drone? Why? / Why not?

2 Do you think it is important to continue to develop drones and improve their design? Why? / Why not?

Drone-free skies

A Vocabulary preview

1 Match the words in bold with the correct definitions.

1	**ban** (v)	a	a process where people try to persuade others to do something
2	**campaign** (n)		
3	**irresponsible** (adj)	b	so unpleasant or painful that you cannot continue doing something
4	**leak** (v)		
5	**presumably** (adv)	c	when a liquid (e.g. water, oil) or gas comes through a hole or a crack
6	**terrifying** (adj)		
7	**unbearable** (adj)	d	to introduce a rule that stops people from doing something
8	**vital** (adj)		

e extremely frightening or scary

f used to say what you think will happen based on what you already know or can guess

g extremely important, essential

h done or said without thinking about the results of your actions or words

2 Complete the sentences with words from Exercise 1. Change the form if necessary.

1 In 30 years, most cars will drive themselves. _____, that means people won't need to take driving lessons.

2 I'd be scared going through a tunnel under the ocean. Water might _____ into the tunnel!

3 The journey to Mars would be completely _____! It would be so boring to be stuck in a small spaceship for nine months.

4 A good, modern transportation system will be _____ to the economic success of this country over the next 20 years.

5 Cars should have built-in speed limits to stop _____ drivers from driving too fast.

6 Local residents have started a _____ to prohibit drone use in the park.

7 The easiest way to make our roads safer would be to _____ motorbikes.

8 I'd never take a train that traveled at a thousand miles an hour. It would be absolutely _____!

3 Work with a partner. Which of the sentences in Exercise 2 do you agree with? Why?

B Before you listen

Look at the picture below. Discuss the questions with a partner.

1 What do you know about drones?

2 What do people use them for?

3 What are some problems connected with drones?

C Global listening

1 🎧 10.1 Listen to *Drone-free skies*. Number the topics in the order that the speakers discuss them. There is one topic that they don't mention.

___ The potential for future problems

___ An accident involving a drone

___ The problem with rules and regulations

___ The noise that drones make

___ The need to train drone pilots

___ The safety record of drones

___ A job that drones can do but people can't

___ Concerns about privacy

2 Work with a partner to discuss what you remember from the radio program.

1 What did Angela Lewis say about the topics from Exercise 1?

2 What did Victor Young say about them?

Listening for bias

D Close listening

Bias means allowing your personal opinions to prevent you from discussing something in a balanced or fair way. Types of bias include:

1 **Selection of facts:** Presenting only facts that support one side of an argument, and ignoring other facts.

2 **Labeling:** Choosing strongly positive or negative names for things instead of more neutral names.

3 **Exaggeration:** Saying something is better or worse than it really is.

4 **Emphasis:** Using strong words like "absolutely," and "extremely."

5 **Repetition:** Saying the same words or ideas several times to make the listener notice and remember them.

🎧 **10.1** Listen to *Drone-free skies* again. Complete the sentences with no more than two words. Then decide how the speakers are showing bias.

1 It's _____ irresponsible.

2 These trouble-makers don't care if their noise _____ destroys other people's lives.

3 It crashed through my son's bedroom window and landed on his _____.

4 But we're talking about a _____ percentage of the total number here.

5 If one of your pipelines starts leaking, it'll take _____ to find the leak.

6 There hasn't been a single death or serious injury involving drones–_____–over the past three years.

7 If we compare that with the safety record of cars, where there are thousands of deaths and injuries every year, it's clear that drones are _____ safe.

8 It was absolutely _____ at the time.

9 But there are _____ of drones out there that aren't harmless.

E Critical thinking

Work with a partner. Discuss the questions.

1 What groups of people might express bias when they speak or write?

2 How can we check whether a speaker is biased? How can we get a more balanced opinion?

Study skills   Planning a persuasive argument

1 **State your position**

   Sum up your argument in one brief, clear sentence.

   You can show that there are strong arguments on more than one side, but indicate which side you find most persuasive.

2 **Support your argument**

   Show why your point of view is good.

   Give evidence (dates, statistics, examples).

3 **Consider your opponents**

   What could your opponents argue?

   How could you persuade listeners that your case and your evidence are better?

© Stella Cottrell (2013)

1 Work with a partner. Use this table to plan a persuasive argument about the future of transportation. Start by choosing the best word to complete the main argument at the top.

Main argument: Twenty years from now, people will travel a lot **more / less** than now.	
Arguments in favor: 1 _____ 2 _____ 3 _____	**Evidence and examples:** 1 _____ 2 _____ 3 _____
Opponent's arguments: 1 _____ 2 _____	**Reasons and evidence:** 1 _____ 2 _____
Why my arguments are stronger. Problems with my opponent's arguments. 1 _____ 2 _____ 3 _____	

2 Work in a group. Discuss the questions.

   1 Why is it necessary to choose which side to support?

   2 Why do you need to support your arguments with evidence and examples?

   3 Why is it useful to predict your opponent's arguments—even if you have no idea what they'll say?

   4 How could you use this technique in other situations, not just formal debates and discussions?

Hyperloops: the fifth form of transportation

A Vocabulary preview

1 Match the words in bold with the correct definitions.

1 Will planes always need an **actual** pilot on board, or will the "pilot" be a computer?

2 Will everything go **smoothly** as we're changing from normal cars to driverless cars, or will there be serious problems?

3 Will it ever be possible to travel around the world using only the **force** of the wind?

4 What do you think the next **revolutionary** form of transportation will be?

5 What will be some **practical** uses of space travel in the future?

6 Will we ever build tunnels thousands of meters below the earth's **surface**?

7 What forms of transportation will stay **basically** the same over the next 100 years?

8 When we travel into space, will we be **literally** weightless, or will it just feel that way?

a (n) the way one object pushes or pulls another object to move it or hold it in place

b (adv) without stress or problems; without sudden changes

c (adj) new and completely changing the way something is done

d (adj) used to emphasize something is real, not a copy

e (adv) used to show that you're telling the truth, without exaggerating or joking

f (adv) in the most important ways

g (adj) useful for real life

h (n) the top or outside layer of something

2 **Work with a partner. Discuss the questions in Exercise 1.**

B Before you listen

Activating prior knowledge

Look at the picture of a Hyperloop on page 177. Work with a partner and discuss the following questions. The words in the glossary box will help you.

1 What can you see in the picture?

2 How do you think Hyperloops work? What drives the pods through the tube?

3 What do you think is special about Hyperloops, compared to other forms of transportation?

4 How do you think Hyperloops deal with the forces of friction and air resistance?

C Global listening

🎧 **10.2** Listen to *Hyperloops: the fifth form of transportation*.
Answer the questions.

1 What does Dr. Demir predict about Hyperloops?

   a They will be just as important in the future as cars, boats, trains, and planes.

   b They are an interesting idea, but they aren't very practical.

   c They are basically the same as trains, but much faster.

2 How do Hyperloops use so little fuel?

   a By using friction to generate their own electricity.

   b By pumping almost all the air out of the tubes.

   c By traveling faster than the speed of sound.

3 What is the biggest challenge, according to Dr. Demir?

   a Turning the magnets on and off very quickly.

   b Making sure the long tubes are safe and strong.

   c Persuading people that Hyperloops are OK.

4 What does Dr. Demir think about her team's chances of winning the competition?

   a They probably won't win because the other teams are very strong.

   b They have an excellent chance of winning.

   c They might get through the first round, but the final round will be hard.

Listening for hyperbole

D Close listening

Hyperbole is an extreme form of exaggeration, when we say that something is much bigger, better, easier, etc., than it really is. People often use hyperbole without thinking, because they are excited or they feel strongly about something. Listen out for words like "basically," which often show that the speaker isn't speaking literally. And even if somebody uses a word like "literally," or "honestly," they might still be using hyperbole!

It was basically the most amazing thing I've ever seen!

The car literally flew down the road at a million miles an hour!

1   🎧 10.2 Listen to *Hyperloops: the fifth form of transportation* again and complete the sentences with no more than two words.

   1   The whole world will be talking about Hyperloops in a few years—they're going to _____!

   2   That means the pods can travel at incredible speeds—much faster than trains, and they use _____ fuel at all.

   3   The train is touching the tracks, so the tracks are _____ against the engine, dragging the train backward.

   4   When you're trying to make a vehicle go fast, air resistance is _____ thing in the world!

   5   You'll be able to travel from one end of the country to the other in _____ at all!

   6   Well, that's actually a fairly simple engineering challenge—a child of five could solve it _____.

   7   For example, how do you ensure there's almost no air in a tube that's _____ miles long?

   8   We've all been working on it _____ a day for the last ten months, and it's been going very well so far.

2   Work with a partner. Try to imagine the truth behind Dr. Demir's hyperbole. What would be a more literal way of describing each topic from Exercise 1?

E Critical thinking

Work with a partner. Discuss the questions.

1   What do you think is the connection between the words "hyperbole," "hypersonic," and "Hyperloop"? Can you think of any other "hyper" words?

2   Do you think Hyperloops will really revolutionize transportation? Why? / Why not?

3   Why do you think universities get involved in competitions like this, even if there's no prize?

Critical thinking

> **Straw man arguments**
>
> During a debate or discussion, speakers sometimes exaggerate their opponent's real arguments, or even invent new arguments for their opponent. They then attack these straw man arguments, in order to make their own arguments seem balanced and reasonable in comparison.

1   Read the extracts from *Drone-free skies*. Discuss the questions with a partner.

The real argument	The straw man argument
Angela: *"The park near my house is very popular with so-called drone pilots, racing their dangerous toys around all day."*	Victor: *"Angela is totally wrong when she claims drones are just silly toys."*
Victor: *"In this country, there hasn't been a single death or serious injury involving drones—not one—over the past three years, and only a handful of minor accidents."*	Angela: *"Presumably, Victor would describe it as another minor accident, not really worth worrying about, but it was absolutely terrifying at the time."*

1   Did Angela really claim that all drones are "just silly toys"?

2   How did Victor make his straw man argument sound like a real argument?

3   Does Victor really think that Angela's accident "isn't worth worrying about"?

4   What technique did Angela use to make this claim sound believable?

2   🎧 10.3 Now listen to three extracts from *Hyperloops: the fifth form of transportation*. Match the extracts with the explanation.

____ Extract 1   ____ Extract 2   ____ Extract 3

a   Dr. Demir treats a neutral comment as a criticism, and then argues against that criticism.

b   Dr. Demir argues against an invented argument based on what people might be thinking.

c   Dr. Demir claims her opponents have an extreme viewpoint, but offers no evidence.

3   Work in a group. Discuss the questions.

1   Why is a straw man a weak form of argument?

2   In what situations do people often use straw man arguments?

3   What can we do when our opponent uses a straw man argument against us?

4   Is it ever OK to use straw man arguments in our own discussions or writing?

Vocabulary development

Vocabulary for transportation and logistics

1 Match the words in bold with the correct definitions.

… we have a **network** of oil pipelines all over the country, … many of which aren't in easily **accessible** places like cities.

We use computers to **steer** the drones, which means the whole process can be controlled by a single engineer in our **headquarters**, hundreds of miles away.

… most drones these days are used for **commercial** reasons – they **distribute** parcels, or look for oil leaks in remote pipelines, or whatever.

It's just a question of getting a computer to turn the magnets on and off **rapidly** to drive the pods forward. It's quite a common form of **motor**.

1 (n) the part of a machine that makes it move or work

2 (adj) used for business purposes

3 (adj) easy to reach, or easy to use

4 (n) a group of people or things which are connected

5 (v) to control the direction a vehicle is traveling

6 (n) the main office of a business or organization

7 (v) to deliver things from one place (e.g. a factory) to many other places (e.g. customers' homes)

8 (adv) quickly, with many changes in a small amount of time

2 Complete the questions with words from Exercise 1. Change the form if necessary.

1 Will the number of people working for logistics companies fall _____ over the next few years? Why? / Why not?

2 What are some of the main _____ uses of drones?

3 How do online stores _____ the products that customers buy on their websites?

4 Which companies have their _____ in your town or city?

5 Does your country have a good _____ of roads and railroads?

6 Apart from vehicles, what are some examples of machines that have electric _____?

7 How do you think people _____ drones? What about Hyperloop pods?

8 Which parts of your university / college are _____ to members of the public?

3 Work with a partner. Discuss the questions in Exercise 2.

Academic words

1 Match the words in bold with the correct definitions.

1 On **behalf** of everybody in the team, I'd like to thank you for all your support this year.

2 Our university is planning to **equip** our library with a new set of computers.

3 The engineers have **assured** us that the test vehicle is safe, so I'm not too worried.

4 I enjoy **manual** jobs from time to time—things like cleaning windows or cutting the grass. It makes a nice change from studying!

5 The drone that we designed kept crashing, so we had to **modify** the design slightly to make the wings longer. Now it works much better.

6 You can't simply claim that drones are dangerous. You need to **justify** your argument by presenting evidence.

a (v) to promise to somebody that something is true, or that it will happen

b (n) as a representative of; in the name of

c (v) to provide somebody or something with useful tools

d (v) to explain why you believe something is fair or right

e (adj) connected with physical work, usually with your hands

f (v) to change something slightly, usually in order to improve it

2 Complete the sentences with words from Exercise 1. Change the form if necessary.

1 Fixing the engine will require time, effort, and _____ skill.

2 Before setting off on a long walk, make sure you're _____ with everything you need, including water, a map, and a satellite phone.

3 If you can't attend the meeting yourself, could you send a co-worker to attend on your _____?

4 I know we're in the airport, but how can they possibly _____ charging $25 for a coffee and a sandwich?

5 I can _____ you that I'll finish the report on time. I promise I won't let you down.

6 I don't think you should change the presentation completely, but why don't you _____ it slightly by changing the order of these two slides?

Speaking model

You are going to learn about the future perfect progressive and language for convincing and making persuasive arguments. You are then going to use these to have a debate about drones.

A Analyze

> **Lucy:** There are many problems with drones, but we'd like to focus on three: drones are noisy, dangerous, and bad for our health. Dan?
>
> **Dan:** Thanks. So, as Lucy says, the first problem is noise. Maybe you think it's not so bad when there's just the occasional drone flying nearby. But when there are thousands of drones flying over your house, keeping you awake all night, what do you think the noise will be like? Believe me: it'll be unbearable.
>
> **Lucy:** That's right. The second problem is safety. Now, our opponents might argue that the drones will be equipped with clever software to steer them away from obstacles. But they're forgetting about birds, which aren't equipped with any software at all! There'll be collisions every five minutes!
>
> **Dan:** Exactly. And the third problem is health. When we have drones delivering our bread, our milk, and our pizzas, we'll no longer have any reason to leave the house. Fifty years from now, we'll have terrible health problems because we'll have been sitting on the sofa for half of our lives! Let's get up from the sofa and walk to the store instead! Let's say no to laziness. Let's say no … to drones.

Read the extract from a formal debate about the future of drones. Then decide if the statements are *T* (True) or *F* (False).

1 Lucy starts with a summary of the arguments that she and Dan will make. T / F
2 Dan explains some advantages and disadvantages of drones.   T / F
3 Lucy and Dan have planned in advance who will argue which points.   T / F
4 Lucy and Dan work will together as a team.   T / F
5 Lucy and Dan end their turn by repeating the three main points.   T / F

B Discuss

Work in a group. Discuss the questions.

1 Do you think the three arguments are persuasive?
2 What do you think about Lucy and Dan's use of hyperbole and straw man arguments?
3 How do you think the second team responded to each argument?
4 What do you think happened next in the debate?

Grammar

Future perfect progressive

We use the future perfect progressive to look back in time from a specific point in the future:

will + have + been + verb + -ing
*The drone **will have been flying** for six hours by the time it arrives.*

There are two main reasons to use the future perfect progressive:

1   To describe the duration of an action up to a specific point in the future:

By the time I finish my thesis, I'll have been working on it <u>for two years</u>.

2   To explain that a future situation will be the result of an earlier process:

I'll be tired when I get home <u>because</u> I'll have been working for 14 hours.

Don't use the future perfect progressive to describe states or completed events. Use the future perfect simple instead.

I'm getting a new cell phone next month. <u>I'll have had</u> my old one for three years by then. (NOT: ~~I'll have been having~~ …)

Let's go to the movies on Friday. <u>I'll have finished</u> my project by then. (NOT: ~~I'll have been finishing~~ …)

---

1   Choose the best tense to complete the sentences.

   1   By the time I arrive at the conference, **I'll have traveled / I'll have been traveling** for over 24 hours. I'll be exhausted!

   2   I'm really looking forward to the weekend. **I'll have done / I'll have been doing** all my exams by then.

   3   My parents have an important wedding anniversary next month: **they'll have been / they'll have been being** married for 25 years.

   4   I don't think I'll join you at the movies tomorrow night. **I'll have studied / I'll have been studying** all day, so I'll probably just want to go to bed.

2   Complete the sentences using the future perfect progressive form of the verb in parentheses.

   1   If one of your pipelines starts leaking, it'll take forever to find the leak. And by the time you finally fix it, _____ (it / leak) for months.

   2   A much bigger challenge will actually be slowing the pods down when they reach their destination. _____ (they / travel) at almost four thousand miles an hour, so if the brakes are too weak, it'll be extremely dangerous.

   3   We'll have 12 months to build an actual working pod. So, it's a long process—by the end, _____ (we / work) on it for nearly two years. But it'll be worth it when we win.

Speaking skill

We use persuasive language when we want to try to change another person's opinion. The most persuasive arguments are based on strong evidence, but our choice of words can also make a big difference:

Sets of three: *Drones are <u>noisy</u>, <u>dangerous</u>, and <u>bad for our health</u>.*

Personalization: *But when there are thousands of drones flying over <u>your</u> house, keeping <u>you</u> awake all night, …*

Rhetorical questions: *<u>What do you think</u> the noise will be like? Believe me: it'll be unbearable.*

Contrasts: *The drones will be <u>equipped with clever software</u>. But birds <u>aren't equipped with any software at all</u>!*

Emotional language and powerful images: *Fifty years from now, <u>we'll have terrible health problems</u> because we'll have been <u>sitting on the sofa for half of our lives</u>!*

Repetition: *<u>Let's say no to</u> laziness. <u>Let's say no to</u> drones.*

1   **Read the sentences and decide which techniques the speakers are using.**

   1   Let's start by addressing that final argument. Not everybody finds it as easy as you do to walk to the store. Think about your own grandparents, or your elderly neighbors … or indeed yourselves, 50 years from now!

   2   And what about people who live in remote areas, who don't even have a nice, accessible store to walk to? For people in such situations, drones could literally be a life-saver.

   3   Because we're not just talking about pizza deliveries here; we're talking about essential drugs and vital medical equipment.

   4   And actually, aren't birds already equipped with a piece of amazing software? It's called … a brain.

   5   As for the noise, let me assure you, Dan, that almost all the drones will be flying well away from your house. The only time you'll hear them is when they come down to your house to deliver your pizzas!

2   **Work with a partner. Make them more persuasive.**

   1   Drones will help us make incredibly detailed and up-to-date maps.

   2   Drones are useful for looking for problems and fixing them.

   3   Drones will be good for the economy.

Pronunciation for speaking

Thought groups

A thought group is a small group of words that communicates a single idea. Speakers pause (/) between thought groups to allow listeners time to think about what's being said. They also stress the key word in each thought group to make their arguments sound more persuasive:

*There are **many** problems with drones / but we'd like to focus on **three** / drones are **noisy** / they're **dangerous** / and they're bad for our **health**.*

Sometimes speakers also add an extra pause (//) in order to draw particular attention to the stressed word after it:

*Let's say **no** to laziness / Let's say **no** // to **drones**.*

1 🎧 **10.4** Divide this extract from the debate into thought groups. Draw a slash (/) between thought groups and underline the stressed word in each. Then listen to compare your ideas with the original.

Let's start by addressing that final argument. Not everybody finds it as easy as you do to walk to the store. Think about your own grandparents or your elderly neighbors or indeed yourselves 50 years from now! And what about people who live in remote areas who don't even have a nice accessible store to walk to? For people in such situations drones could literally be a life-saver. Because we're not just talking about pizza deliveries here; we're talking about essential drugs and vital medical equipment.

2 🎧 **10.5** Look at these sentences from *Drone-free skies* and *Hyperloops: the fifth form of transportation*. Draw a double slash (//) in each sentence where you think the speaker paused for emphasis. Then listen and check.

1 And as the number of drones grows, the potential for serious accidents will increase dramatically.

2 We want to make sure that the skies remain safe for everybody.

3 The whole world will be talking about Hyperloops in a few years—they're going to change everything!

4 I think everyone has a chance—you just need to believe in yourself.

5 But it'll be worth it when we win.

6 Maybe we'll play a small part in making the world a better place.

3 Look back at the persuasive arguments you wrote in Exercise 2 in the Speaking Skill section. Mark the thought groups, pauses and stress. Read them aloud.

Speaking task

Debate the pros and cons of a future trend toward increased commercial drone use.

Brainstorm

Work in groups. Brainstorm some positive and negative effects of drone use in the future.

Plan

Twenty years from now, our skies will be filled with drones. This will be bad for society and cannot be allowed to happen.

Divide your group into two teams.

Team 1: You agree with the statement above.

Team 2: You disagree with the statement above.

In your team, make a list of four or five ideas to support your position. Think about what language you could use to make your arguments more persuasive and where you might use thought groups.

Speak

Hold your debate. Challenge your opponents if they use hyperbole or present straw man arguments.

Share

Report back to the class on what you discussed. What were the most persuasive arguments?

Reflect

Work with a partner. Discuss the questions.

1   What do you really think? Will the world be better or worse when there are drones everywhere?

2   What do you think about Hyperloops? And other new forms of transportation?

3   What do you think about the use of bias, hyperbole, and straw man arguments? Are they useful ways of persuading people? Or should we always avoid them?

Review

Wordlist

MACMILLAN DICTIONARY

Vocabulary preview

actual (adj) ***	force (n) ***	practical (adj) ***	surface (n) ***
ban (v) **	irresponsible (adj)	presumably (adv) **	terrifying (adj)
basically (adv) **	leak (v) *	revolutionary (adj) **	unbearable (adj)
campaign (n) ***	literally (adv) **	smoothly (adv)	vital (adj) ***

Vocabulary development

accessible (adj)	distribute (v) **	motor (n) ***	rapidly (adv)
commercial (adj) ***	headquarters (n) **	network (n) ***	steer (v) *

Academic words

assure (v) *	equip (v) **	manual (adj) *
behalf (n) **	justify (v) **	modify (v) *

Academic words review

Complete the sentences using words from the box.

assure	compensated	contrast	justify	modified

1 The colors on the TV set are too bright. You need to adjust the _____.

2 The designers _____ the controls of the car so that disabled drivers could use it.

3 The judge decided that the accident was not the victim's fault and _____ him for his injuries.

4 "I'm not sure what else I can say to _____ you", he said quietly.

5 It's becoming increasingly difficult to _____ such an expense.

Unit review

Listening 1		I can listen for the speaker's bias.
Listening 2		I can listen for hyperbole.
Study skill		I can plan a persuasive argument.
Vocabulary		I can use vocabulary of transportation and logistics.
Grammar		I can use the future perfect progressive.
Speaking		I can use language to convince and make persuasive arguments.

Student role cards

Unit 8, Speaking task, page 150

"Listen, everyone involved in the film making process needs to get paid, which they won't if people don't pay for the content. To put it simply, if piracy continues unchecked it will lead to the death of the industry." – *Jess Harrington, actor*

"Whatever way you look at it, piracy is a crime and needs to be addressed." – *Scott Hernandez, writer and producer*

"I don't worry about people who download one movie and watch it at home with friends. But downloading films on a large scale and distributing them through your own website—well, that's no different than robbing a bank." – *Omar Akidil, producer*

"Piracy is not a victimless crime."
– *Text shown at the beginning of DVDs*

"I don't think the average person realizes just how much damage they're doing to the movie industry by downloading content illegally." – *Junpei Tanaka, writer*

"The success of Spotify and Netflix proves that if you provide instant access to high-quality content at an affordable price, people will pay for it rather than steal it."
– *Alex Washington, actor*

"Piracy is nothing new. People used to record films straight from the TV onto VHS tapes and that didn't kill the industry. I don't see why downloading films is any different." – *Oscar Lindström, modern history lecturer at Pembrook State*

"We need to differentiate between piracy on a corporate or commercial level, like what people are doing in their homes for their own use. This kind of file sharing, though unauthorized, probably doesn't impact sales in a big way." – *Rebecca Sharp, media analyst*

"People who download films illegally for their own profit deserve heavy fines. But putting them in jail with violent criminals is cruel and unusual punishment, in my view."
– *Yasmina Bolt, defense attorney*

"Illegal downloading will continue as long as anti-piracy laws are ineffective and existing technology makes pirating so easy. Human nature is what it is. The threat of punishment doesn't deter anyone."
– *Carl Kovacs, software engineer*

Functional language phrase bank

The phrases below give common ways of expressing useful functions. Use them to help you as you're completing the *Discussion points*, *Critical thinking* activities, and *Speaking* tasks.

Asking for clarification
Sorry, can you explain that some more?
Could you say that another way?
When you say … do you mean …?
Sorry, I don't follow that.
What do you mean?

Asking for repetition
Could you repeat that, please?
I'm sorry, I didn't catch that.
Could you say that again?

When you don't know the word for something
What does … mean?
Sorry, I'm not sure what … means.

Working with a partner
Would you like to start?
Shall I go first?
Shall we do this one first?
Where do you want to begin?

Giving opinions
I think that …
It seems to me that …
In my opinion …
As I see it …

Agreeing and disagreeing
I know what you mean.
That's true.
You have a point there.
Yes. I see what you're saying, but …
I understand your point, but …
I don't think that's true.

Asking for opinions
Do you think …?
Do you feel …?
What do you think about …?
How about you, Jennifer?
What do you think?
What about you?
Does anyone have any other ideas?
Do you have any thoughts on this?

Asking for more information
In what way?
Why do you think that?
Can you give an example?

Not giving a strong preference
It doesn't matter to me.
I don't really have a strong preference.
I've never really thought about that.
Either is fine.

Expressing interest
I'd like to hear more about that.
That sounds interesting.
How interesting!
Tell me more about that.

Giving reasons
This is … because …
This has to be … because …
I think … because …

Checking understanding
Do you know what I mean?
Do you see what I'm saying?
Are you following me?

Putting things in order
This needs to come first because …
I think this is the most / least important because …
For me, this is the most / least relevant because …

Academic words revision

Units 1–5

Complete the sentences using the words in the box. Change the form if necessary.

> attain context contrast detect emerge
> identify occupy strategy submit visual

1   FMV is an award-winning _____ effects company based in London.
2   A new species of spider has been _____ in northern Australia.
3   Candidates must _____ their proposals by June 8.
4   She watched in terror as a crocodile _____ from the water.
5   The defendant claimed his remarks had been taken out of _____.
6   The device can _____ slight changes in blood pressure.
7   The exchange highlighted an obvious _____ between the two cultures.
8   Despite his illness, Hassan still managed to _____ six A grades.
9   Studying seems to _____ all of my time in the evenings.
10 We need to develop a clearer marketing _____ for South East Asia.

Units 6–10

Complete the sentences using the words in the box. Change the form if necessary.

> appreciate conclude economy eliminate equip
> expose justify manual reinforce transform

1   The company claim their product _____ toxins in the body.
2   Over the last decade, social media has _____ the way we communicate.
3   If you've got time, I'd really _____ some help with this.
4   There's an increasing demand for skilled _____ workers.
5   Commuters are _____ to dangerously high levels of pollution.
6   Critics argue it could have a negative impact on the global _____.
7   It's important to _____ yourself properly before starting the climb.
8   I realise you were angry, but that doesn't _____ your behavior.
9   The article aims to _____ the view that fracking is dangerous.
10 The report _____ that digital devices have little impact on performance.

Citations

p47 (Track 3.1) – Source: Pew Research Center survey 'Mobile Access Shifts Social Media Use and Other Online Activities' Sept. 25–Oct. 9, 2014, and Feb. 10–Mar. 16, 2015

p51 (Track 3.2) – Source: Wired [online] 'Author Nicholas Carr: The Web Shatters Focus, Rewires Brains' 24.05.10

p62 (Infographic) – Source: WHO [online] 'Household air pollution and health' 01.02.16

p101 (Track 6.1) – Source: NBC News [online] 'Airplane air: not as bad as you think' 13.01.10

p137 (Track 8.1) – Source: Norton [online] 'What is cybercrime?' Accessed: 25.07.16

p137 (Track 8.1) – Source: Security Intelligence [online] '20 Eye-Opening Cybercrime Statistics' 14.11.16

p137 (Track 8.1) – Source: The National Academic Press 'Computers at Risk: Computing in the Information age' (1991)

p141 (Track 8.2) – Source: USA.gov 'Identity Theft' Accessed: 25.07.17

p141 (Critical thinking) – Source: The BMJ 'Aircraft noise and cardiovascular disease near Heathrow airport in London: small area study' BMJ 2013;347:f5432

Macmillan Education
4 Crinan Street
London N1 9XW

A division of Springer Nature Limited
Companies and representatives throughout the world

ISBN 978-1-380-00595-3

Text, design and illustration © Springer Nature Limited 2018
Written by Ellen Kisslinger and Lida Baker
Unit 10 written by Jeremy Day
Series Consultant Dorothy E. Zemach

The authors have asserted their right to be identified as the authors of this work in accordance with the Copyright, Designs and Patents Act 1988.

This edition published 2018
First edition entitled "Skillful" published 2012 by Springer Nature Limited

All rights reserved. No part of this publication may be reproduced, stored in a retrieval system, or transmitted in any form or by any means, electronic, mechanical, photocopying, recording, or otherwise, without the prior written permission of the publishers.

Designed by emc design ltd
Illustrated by Carl Morris (Beehive Illustration) pp40, 96; emc design ltd
Cover design by emc design ltd
Cover picture by Sam Parij (Eye Candy Illustration)/Getty Images/Moment Open/ Alicia Llop
Picture research by Julie-anne Wilce

Authors' acknowledgements

Ellen Kisslinger
I would like to thank the Macmillan Education team for their support and guidance in the effort to address the academic needs of students through this course. Special thanks to my daughter, Rachel Belanger, for her research assistance and willingness to share her insights.

Lida Baker
Loving thanks go to my husband Paul for his endless support and patience as I was working on this book.

The publishers would like to thank the following for their thoughtful insights and perceptive comments during the development of the material:

Dalal Al Hitty University of Bahrain, Bahrain; Karin Heuert Galvão, i-Study Interactive Learning, São Paulo, Brazil; Ohanes Sakris Australian College of Kuwait, Kuwait; Eoin Jordan, Xi'an Jiaotong Liverpool University, Suzhou, China; Aaron Rotsinger, Xi'an Jiaotong-Liverpool University, Suzhou, China; Dr. Osman Z. Barnawi, Royal Commission Colleges and Institutes, Yanbu, Saudi Arabia; Andrew Lasher, SUNY Korea, Incheon, South Korea; Fatoş Uğur Eskiçırak, Bahçeşehir University, Istanbul, Turkey; Dr. Asmaa Awad, University of Sharjah, Sharjah, United Arab Emirates; Amy Holtby The Petroleum Institute, Abu Dhabi, United Arab Emirates, Dr. Christina Gitsaki, Zayed University, Dubai, United Arab Emirates.

The authors and publishers would like to thank the following for permission to reproduce their photographs:

Alamy/blickwinkel pp62(t),63(t), Alamy/cm studio p28(bcr), Alamy/Stuart Cox p155(bl), Alamy/dpa picture alliance pp26(t),27(t), Alamy/Goran Šafarek p105(tc), Alamy/SOURCENEXT p11(b), Alamy/jeremy sutton-hibbert p124(b), Alamy/ Jochen Tack pp152(t),153(t); **Getty Images**/adamkaz p51(b), Getty images/AFP/ ARL DE SOUZA p130(b), Getty Images/blackred p141(br), Getty Images/Bloomberg pp80(t),81(t), Getty images/Alexandr Bognat p28(bl), Getty Images/Andrew Brookes pp134(t),135(t), Getty Images/Bulgac p28(br), Getty Images/caristo p155(br), Getty Images/Cultura RM Exclusive/Colin Hawkins p109(b), Getty Images/Design Pics/ Ron Nickel p105(tl), Getty Images/FRED DUFOUR pp116(t),117(t), Getty Images/ edia for Medical pp98(t),99(t), Getty Images/Sean Ellis p15(b), Getty Images/ Roger Eritja p154(bl), Getty Images/ferrantraite p55(b), Getty Images/Lijuan Guo Photography p65(b), Getty Images/Izabela Habur p83(b), Getty Images/Hinterhaus Productions p113(b), Getty Images/Dan Kitwood p119(b), Getty Images/Morsa Images p104(t), Getty Images/Mint Images/Frans Lanting p69(b), Getty Images/ Richard Newstead p37(b), Getty Images/Greg Pease p9(t), Getty Images/Dan Porges p155(cr), Getty Images/Jim Purdum p47(b), Getty Images/ Joe Raedle p137(b), Getty Images/Andreas Rentz pp35,173(b),(b), Getty Images/SCIENCE PHOTO LIBRARY/STEVE GSCHMEISSNER p102(b), Getty Images/shironosov p13(b), Getty Images/Squaredpixels p159(b), Getty Images/Stephen St. John p77(b), Getty Images/Stringer/Nigel Roddis p87(b), Getty Images/Stringer/REMKO DE WAAL p33(b), Getty Images/ Universal History Archive p167(b), Getty Images/Westend61 pp32,122(bl),(bl); **Science Photo Library** pp44(t),45(t), Science Photo Library/ CLAUS LUNAU p77(b); **Shutterstock**/Jubal Harshaw p106(b), Shutterstock/ Hinochika p108(bl), Shutterstock/M. Unal Ozmen p28(bcl), Shutterstock/Puffin's Pictures p105(tr); **Superstock**/Blend Images pp170(t)171(t); **Thomson Reuters** pp8,26,44,62,80,98, 116,134,152,170(bl),(bl),(bl),(bl),(bl),(bl),(bl),(bl),(bl),(bl), Thomson Reuters/Courtesy Wyss Institute at Harvard University, Courtesy Octo Telematics, Courtesy TV Globo.

Printed and bound in Poland by CGS
2023 2022 2021 2020 2019
14 13 12 11 10 9 8 7 6

PALGRAVE STUDY SKILLS

by bestselling author, **Stella Cottrell**

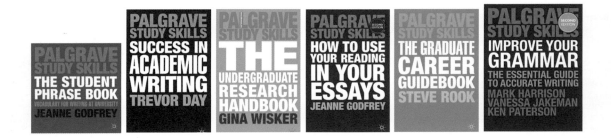

palgravestudyskills.com

facebook.com/skills4study

twitter.com/skills4study